...urned on or before the last date stamped below.

AS Level for AQA

Travel & Tourism

Peter Hayward • Alan Marvell • Hayley Reynolds

www.heinemann.co.uk
✓ Free online support
✓ Useful weblinks
✓ 24 hour online ordering

01865 888058

Inspiring generations

Heinemann Educational Publishers
Halley Court, Jordan Hill, Oxford OX2 8EJ
Part of Harcourt Education

Heinemann is a registered trademark of
Harcourt Education Limited

© Alan Marvell, Peter Hayward, Hayley Reynolds

First published 2005

09 08 07 06 05
10 9 8 7 6 5 4 3 2 1

British Library Cataloguing in Publication Data is available
from the British Library on request.

10-digit ISBN 0 435 44657 6
13-digit ISBN 978 0 435 44657 4

9700000 239

Typeset and illustrated by ⋌ Tek-Art, Croydon, Surrey

Original illustrations © Harcourt Education Limited 2005
Cover design by Wooden Ark Studios
Printed by Bath Colourbooks
Cover photo: © Robert Harding

Contents

Acknowledgements

The publishers wish to thank the following for their kind permission to reproduce the photos in this book.

Alamy 95, 101, 128, 130, 130, 136 (bottom); Alamy/Travel Ink 97 (bottom left); Alamy/Travel Shots 14; BAE Systems 112; Britainonview/Ingrid Rasmussen 36; Butlins 21; Corbis 2 (bottom right), 16, 20, 44, 59, 99, 102, 119, 134, 135; easyJet 31; Getty Images/Photodisc 94 (bottom left and right), 96, 97 (bottom right), 136 (top); Harcourt Education Ltd/Debbie Rowe 11; Jane Hance 58; Lonely Planet Images 2 (bottom left), 19, 129; Rex Features 35

Every effort has been made to contact copyright holders of material reproduced in this book. Any omissions will be rectified in subsequent printings if notice is given to the publishers.

Introduction

Travel and tourism is one of the world's fastest growing industries, with over two million people employed in tourism-related industries in the UK. The AS GCE Travel and Tourism (Single Award) has been designed as a qualification that provides knowledge and understanding of this dynamic industry. The qualification will enable you to progress to qualifications in further and higher education, training or employment.

This book has been produced to meet the requirements of the AQA AS GCE Travel and Tourism (Single Award) qualification. It has been specifically written by a team of experienced authors to enable you to get the most from your course.

The book is set out in the order of the units that you will be studying:

* Unit 1 Inside Travel and Tourism

* Unit 2 Travel and Tourism – A People Industry

* Unit 3 Travel Destinations.

Each unit in this book provides you with essential information that you need to know, along with a range of features, which are listed below:

* **Key terms** – these provide concise definitions of important words and phrases.

* **Case study** – these are detailed examples to show you how key ideas relate to the travel and tourism industry.

* **Think about it** – these provide you with an opportunity to think, discuss and reflect on important questions affecting the industry.

* **Skills practice** – these allow you to research and investigate ideas related to the information that has been discussed and to begin working towards your portfolio.

* **Knowledge check** – these allow you to check your understanding of what you have learnt before you start work on your portfolio.

How will I study?

You will research and investigate a wide range of issues relating to travel and tourism. These will be based around a series of assignments that are agreed with your tutor. You will be expected to use a variety of different sources, some of which can include:

* Libraries and information centres

* Internet searches

* Travel brochures and guidebooks

* News reports and advertisements from a variety of different media

* Visiting and talking to people in the travel and tourism industry

* Using industry reports and trade journals

* Learning from guest speakers

* If possible, work experience with a travel and tourism company.

How will I be assessed?

Two-thirds of the qualification is assessed by a portfolio of activities that are set out in the AQA specification. Your tutor will give you a copy. The portfolio is based on coursework and other activities as specified by your tutor. You must make sure that you follow the instructions carefully and that the portfolio is all your own work. This book provides you with examples and suggestions on where to find information.

The other third of the qualification is a test that contains short-answer and extended-answer questions. This book prepares you for the test with hints, suggestions and practice questions.

We hope you enjoy using this book and good luck with your course.

UNIT 1

Inside travel and tourism

Introduction

This unit introduces you to travel and tourism. You will learn that the travel and tourism industry is complex and diverse and is made up of a large number of different organisations. You will also discover that organisations in the industry are interrelated and interdependent. You will investigate the development and growth of travel and tourism and the roles of the different sectors of the travel and tourism industry.

This unit provides the foundation for supporting the more detailed study of the travel and tourism industry in other GCE units, as well as an overview of the nature and growth of the UK travel and tourism industry.

How you will be assessed

Assessment for this unit is through an externally assessed written paper. The paper will be two hours long and will comprise short and extended answer questions.

To help you prepare for the written paper you will need to study at least two destinations in the UK and overseas.

Throughout the unit, activities and tasks will help you to learn and remember information in preparation for your external assessment.

After studying this unit you need to have learned:

✳ To define travel and tourism and know the main types of tourism
✳ To understand the nature of the travel and tourism industry
✳ To be able to describe the main historical developments and factors that have led to the growth of the industry into its current characteristics
✳ To be able to identify the roles of the different sectors of the travel and tourism industry
✳ To understand the areas of overlap and the nature of the relationships between sectors within the travel and tourism industry.

Defining travel and tourism

Two weeks in the sun; a business trip to see customers; visiting relatives in Australia. All of these are examples of travel and tourism activities and there are a variety of organisations involved in supplying travel and tourism products and services to customers.

This section aims to examine what is meant by travel and tourism, the different parts of the industry and the range of tourism destinations travellers visit.

In the section you will learn:

* The main types of tourism
* The main reasons people travel
* Different types of travel and tourism products and services
* The size of and role of organisations in the industry
* The industry is dominated by commercial organisations
* The support and influence of public and voluntary organisations within the industry
* Internal and external pressures on the industry
* The impact of travel and tourism activities on destinations and host communities.

What are travel and tourism?

Travel and *tourism* is concerned with people travelling away from home on a temporary basis – i.e. they intend to return home at a given point in time. The reasons people choose to travel are varied and these shall be examined later in this section. The destinations people travel to are also varied and range from UK seaside resorts to exotic, little-visited faraway places.

A traditional UK seaside resort and an exotic overseas beach location

The demand for travel and tourism products and services has created a large and dynamic industry that continues to grow. Covering a number of activities and organisations, travel is seen as the key component in the industry as it concerns how people actually get to their chosen destination and how they travel around the area they are visiting. Without travel there would be no tourism and without tourism there would be little demand for travel services.

Key terms

Travel Travel is concerned with how people get to their chosen destination and how they travel around the area they are visiting.

Tourism Tourism is 'the temporary, short-term movement of people to destinations outside the places where they normally live and work and the activities they take part in during their stay at those destinations.' (*Tourism Society*, 1976)

Think about it

In groups of three or four, list as many methods of transport as you can think of. Then consider the advantages and disadvantages of each method.

Skills practice

1 Visit your local tourist information office to collect information about five different local tourist attractions.

2 Imagine you are working at promoting your local area. Prepare a PowerPoint presentation selling the local attractions you have collected information on to attract visitors to the area.

Are we coming or going?

Tourism can be classified into three main types:

* Domestic

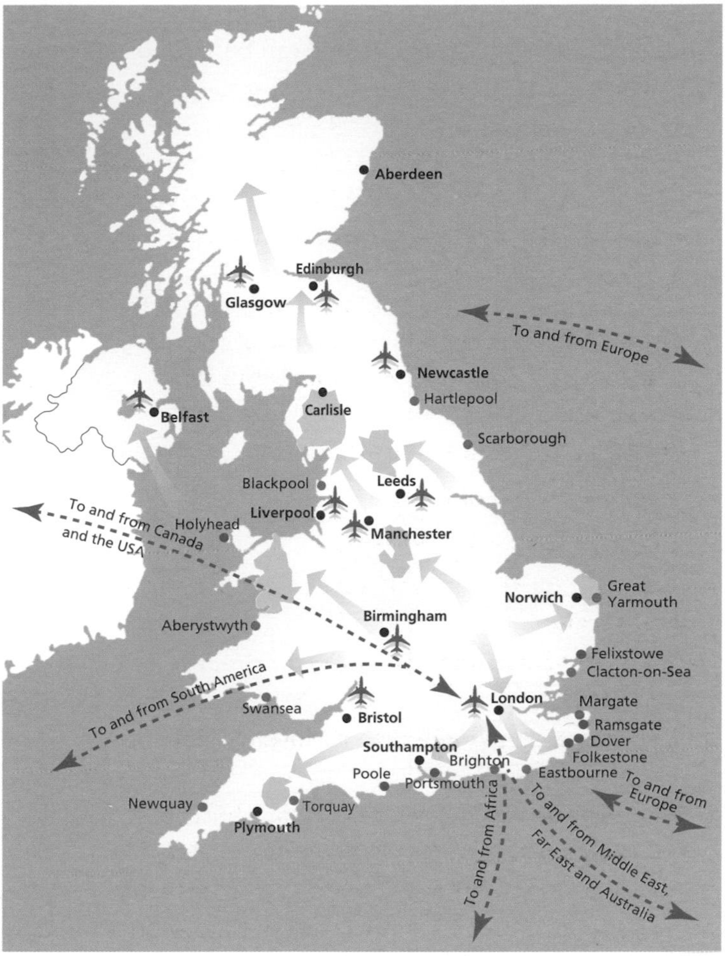

Figure 1.1 The UK's main flows of tourism

* Inbound
* Outbound.

Domestic tourism involves UK residents visiting locations within the UK either for a day trip, visiting friends or relatives, or for a holiday. The UK has a wealth of many towns and cities that attract tourists every year.

Skills practice

1 Write a list of as many places as you can think of in the UK which attract tourists to visit them.

2 Compare this list with a colleague who has also completed Task 1.

3 Draw a large outline (possibly big enough for a wall display) of a map of the UK. On to this map, mark all the UK tourist spots you identified in Tasks 1 and 2.

The UK, even though only a small country, has different types of destinations that can be visited by tourists.

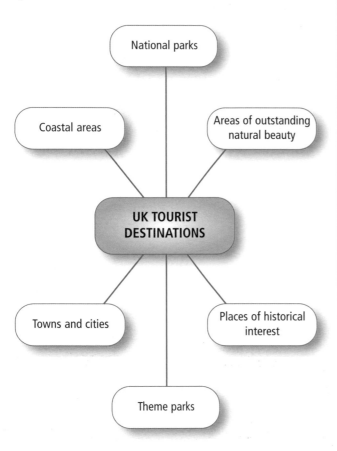

Figure 1.2 The range of UK tourist destinations

For each of the above types of UK tourist destination, you need to be able to name different destinations for each type. Using your own knowledge and a map of the UK to help you, create a list of five destinations for each category.

ICT can be used to help you with this task, either for research purposes or presenting your findings.

As part of your external examination, you need to be able to interpret and analyse data collected on the travel and tourism industry. The next activity contains data about the most visited places in the UK. This is a great opportunity to practise your skills of interpretation and analysis for your examination.

National Tourist Board regions	Number of trips made by UK residents (millions) in 1996	Number of trips made by UK residents (millions) in 2002
United Kingdom	154.2	167.3
Northumbria	3.7	4.8
Cumbria	3.7	4.3
North West	11.9	14.5
Yorkshire	11.9	12.2
East of England	15.8	14.5
Heart of England	18.9	24.6
London	12.9	16.1
Southern	11.5	14.6
South East England	11.9	10.9
South West	17.5	21.0
England	117.3	134.9
Wales	13.6	11.9
Scotland	19.6	18.5
Northern Ireland	3.8	2.8

Source: United Kingdom Tourism Survey, sponsored by the National Tourist Boards; International Passenger Survey, Office for National Statistics

1 What is the above data showing? (2 marks)

2 From 1996 to 2002, some areas of the UK have experienced an increase in the number of visitors to their area. Identify two of these areas. (2 marks)

3 The East of England is an area of the UK that has seen a decrease in the number of visitors between 1996 and 2002. As a hotel owner in Norwich (which is in the East of England), these figures have concerned you. What could you do as the hotel owner to try and attract tourists, and their money, to the area? (6 marks)

4 What factors do you think have contributed to the general increase in the number of visits made from 1996 to 2002? (6 marks)

5 Calculate the percentage change in number of visitors from 1996 to 2002 for London and Wales. (4 marks)

6 These figures show that overall there has been an increase in domestic tourism between 1996 and 2002. Despite the increase, what do you think are the challenges facing organisations involved in the domestic travel and tourism industry? (8 marks)

CASE STUDY

Mary, Ray and their friends

Mary and Ray are both in their seventies and have been retired for a number of years. They enjoy visiting Spain and the Canary Islands in the cold winter months for the sunshine and warmth. However, through the rest of the year Mary, Ray and several of their friends take pleasure in going on several trips to various UK destinations. Their trips take them all over the UK and last for five days, usually starting on a Monday and finishing on a Friday. They travel on organised coach tours. Recent places they have visited include Blackpool, Edinburgh, Truro and Eastbourne.

1 **Mary, Ray and their friends are part of an increasing group of senior citizens who have money to spend on travel and tourism. What do you think are the requirements of such travellers?**
2 **Most of Mary and Ray's holidays are organised group trips. Why do you think they prefer this to travelling alone?**
3 **Imagine you are working for 'Speedies', an organisation which specialises in coach trips for the over 65s. Choose a UK destination and conduct some research to plan a five-day holiday itinerary for Mary, Ray and their friends. You need to find a hotel with bed, breakfast and evening meal options, plan three-day trips and nightly evening entertainment.**

Inbound tourism

When you visit another country you are an *inbound tourist* to whichever country you are visiting. Therefore, visitors from other countries to the UK are inbound tourists. The UK is popular with inbound tourists and particularly with visitors from the USA due to the history and culture of this country. The idea of visiting royal palaces and castles and the birthplaces of famous writers such as Shakespeare, is a magnet to many inbound tourists.

Think about it

What makes the UK attractive to overseas visitors?

Skills practice

1 Prepare a questionnaire which includes questions about where travellers to a particular area have originated from. Include questions that will help you to discover where the traveller started their journey, how they travelled, why they are visiting a particular area and how long they are planning to spend in that area.

2 Visit an airport, railway station or bus station close to where you live to survey people who have just arrived at that destination to find out where they have come from. Use the questionnaire you prepared in Task 1 and remember to ask the permission of both individuals and the authorities of where you plan to survey travellers.

3 Analyse your results to draw conclusions about the origins of travellers. Use ICT to help present your findings in a professional manner. Analysis must also be numerical as well as written so use bar charts and pie charts etc. to illustrate your findings.

CASE STUDY

The Braithwaites

John and Colleen Braithwaite live in a suburb about twenty miles southeast of Sydney in New South Wales, Australia. John and Colleen have taken early retirement after selling their hardware business, which they ran for many years. After having spent several months travelling around Australia, they now want to visit the UK and Europe. John and Colleen have visited Europe before but only for a short period of time. They now wish to spend three months visiting the UK and continental Europe.

1   John and Colleen are inbound tourists. In your own words what does this mean?

2   Suggest two ways John and Colleen could book their tour to the UK and Europe. For the two suggestions you make, consider the advantages and disadvantages of using those methods.

3   As inbound tourists John and Colleen contribute to the UK economy in many ways. How do you think they will contribute to the UK economy?

4   John and Colleen want to visit London as part of their trip. They have three days in the capital and want to visit at least five cultural tourist attractions. Use the Internet to plan an itinerary for John and Colleen based on their requirements.

Skills practice

The UK is often very expensive for inbound tourists to visit. This is due in part to the high cost of living in the UK but is also due to the value of the pound and exchange rates. Carry out some research to answer the following questions, remembering that textbooks are also a great way to find out information, as is the Internet:

1   What are exchange rates?

2   If the value of the pound is high, what impact will this have on the number of tourists visiting the UK from overseas?

3   How can UK destinations and tourism agencies attract overseas visitors and overcome the problem of the UK being perceived as an expensive place to holiday in?

Outbound tourism

Leaving the UK in search of warmer weather and sunnier climes makes people outbound tourists. *Outbound tourism* involves UK residents leaving the UK and spending their holidays (and their money) in another country. Money spent by outbound tourists benefits the economies of the countries they visit and provides jobs and wages for local people.

In recent years, UK tourists have become much more adventurous in their choices of overseas destinations. In the 1950s and 1960s, the majority of outbound tourists from the UK would visit the Mediterranean resorts in Spain, such as Benidorm, Torremolinos and Lloret de Mar. During the 1980s, America and in particular the 'Sunshine State' of Florida became popular with UK tourists. The 1990s saw a growth in short-stay visits to cities and resorts in the Caribbean and the Far East, and South America also became popular.

The majority of destinations visited by tourists from the UK are accessed by air travel. Holidays involve either *short-haul* flights or *long-haul* flights. The distinction between the two is the length of flight needed to reach a particular destination. Short-haul flights usually take less than five hours and include destinations such as Greece, Spain, Portugal and other parts of Europe. Traditionally, short-haul destinations have been the major market for UK tourists visiting overseas, however the long-haul destinations have stolen some market share in recent years, as discussed earlier. Long-haul destinations take more than five hours to reach by air and this is the fastest growing segment of the holiday market.

Skills practice

You are a writer for a local newspaper and have been asked to contribute to the next edition's travel section. You have to write about the attractions of one long-haul destination from a choice of the Dominican Republic, Goa or Hong Kong. You need to include the following details:

•   Where in the world the destination is

•   How long it takes to reach the destination

•   Attractions of that destination.

Just like domestic tourists, outbound tourists are looking for a holiday to suit their own individual requirements and this has been a contributing factor in the variety and number of resorts visited by UK outbound tourists.

Skills practice

You are to imagine that you are working in a local travel agency and a variety of different customers have been to see you about finding a resort that would be suitable for their particular needs. Read the following descriptions and suggest resorts for these groups of people, stating why the resorts would be suitable.

1 Anne is a nineteen-year-old university student who wishes to go on holiday in the summer with five other friends who are the same age. The girls have a limited budget of £400 each and want to go away for one week only. The girls also want lazy days sunbathing and a resort with good nightlife.

2 James is an old romantic and wants to take his wife away for a surprise anniversary trip. Ideally, James would like to visit a city in Europe which is rich in culture, has good restaurants and breathtaking sights.

3 Steve and Vicky are intrepid travellers and each year try to visit a country they have never visited before. This year the couple have saved hard and have three weeks off work. They also like to take part in new and extreme sports. Over the last five years they have travelled to America, Italy, China, Mexico and France.

Skills practice

For your external examination you need to be able to interpret statistical information on types of tourism. Using your research skills, visit the website of the Office of National Statistics to find data on the most popular overseas destinations visited by UK tourists. Once you have collected this data, you can write a report showing your findings, using these guidelines:

- Which countries do UK tourists like to visit?

- Why do you think these resorts are popular?

- Do you think these destinations will still be as popular in ten years' time?

Why do people travel?

People travel for leisure, for business or to visit friends or relatives. These are the three main reasons people choose to travel. For each of these reasons, tourism can be domestic, inbound or outbound. For example, a group of friends visiting the Lake District for a weekend of walking would be classed as domestic tourists and the reason behind their trip would be leisure. Directors from a Japanese company who have opened a factory in the UK would be inbound tourists visiting the UK on business purposes. A brother and his wife visiting a relative who lives in New Zealand would be outbound tourists and the purpose of their visit is visiting friends and family.

Different reasons for travel mean that tourists have different needs and requirements based upon the purpose of their travel. A businessman when visiting London on a business trip may wish to stay in a hotel with conference facilities and which is close to an airport to receive international guests. However, the same businessman will have very different requirements when he visits London for the weekend with his family. He may want to stay in a hotel that is in the centre of London, close to all the main attractions, and which offers family rooms and children's meals. Therefore, the same tourist has very different requirements depending on the reason or purpose of his travel.

Leisure tourism

For many people, travelling away from home for a temporary period is for *leisure* purposes. Summer holidays, day trips to the seaside, shopping expeditions, all have leisure as the underlying reason. Holidays for leisure purposes can be classified into several categories.

Figure 1.3 Categories of leisure holidays

Sightseeing and visiting attractions, whilst not strictly holidays, are still tourism activities with leisure at their core.

Visiting friends or relatives

People today are more mobile than they have ever been. We move around the country and the world for work and therefore have *friends and relatives* living in different geographical areas. In 2001, this type of tourism accounted for 25 per cent of all holidays taken by UK tourists.

A beach holiday at home or abroad is one of the most popular leisure activities among UK tourists

Visiting loved ones and those close to you usually has one major advantage – free accommodation. Because of this tourists visiting friends and family tend to spend money saved on eating out, visiting leisure facilities and travelling around the area.

CASE STUDY
Travelling around the UK

Giovanni and Helen have lived in Leeds for the last three years. The couple met at university and after having lived in London for several years, and working hard and playing even harder, decided to move to be close to family.

Helen is from the Leeds area originally but Giovanni is from Brighton. The couple, wanting to settle down and start a family, felt that they wanted to be near to one set of family to help and support them. House prices were cheaper in the north and this swayed their decision to move to Leeds.

Most weekends, Helen and Giovanni either travel to stay with family or friends or have guests at their home. Their university friends live in different parts of the country especially between Nottingham and Bristol.

1 Why do Helen and Giovanni travel to certain parts of the country at weekends?
2 If friends and family visit Helen and Giovanni in Leeds, they do not have to pay for accommodation. How do these visitors contribute to the local economy of Leeds if they are not paying to stay in hotels?
3 Leeds is a very popular city and attracts many visitors because of its shopping attractions. It also has many cultural attractions such as the Royal Armouries. Conduct some research to find out about this attraction and suggest to Helen and Giovanni whether or not it is worth visiting.

Business tourism

Travel and tourism is not just for leisure and pleasure purposes. Many people have to travel as part of their jobs and this travel can be international as well as national. With a global economy, many companies operate in more than one country and employees may be required to visit other parts of the business in different countries.

Business travel is often quite luxurious, with first-class travel and accommodation in the best hotels. It may also often be viewed as a perk of a job and a real bonus.

Business people need to travel for several reasons. These may include:

* business meetings
* exhibitions and trade fairs
* conferences and conventions.

Skills practice

You work for a travel agent that specialises in making travel arrangements for local business people. An architect has approached you to organise a business trip for herself and three other colleagues to the Ideal Home Exhibition at the NEC in Birmingham. You need to:

* make travel arrangements by rail from your local railway station
* book tickets for the exhibition
* find overnight accommodation in Birmingham
* book a table for an evening meal at a top Birmingham restaurant
* fully cost the whole trip for the four architects.

CASE STUDY
Business travel

Phil Reynolds works as a Store Planner for Marks & Spencer Plc. Phil's job role is varied and his work takes him all over the UK and the Republic of Ireland (Eire). As a result, Phil travels a lot.

Phil's job role is primarily to design the interior and layout of Marks & Spencer stores. This ranges from refitting and refurbishing older stores to designing the layout and look of brand new stores for the company. Phil works as a member of a small team who between them look after all of the company's 360 stores.

Marks & Spencer Plc has had stores in Eire since the late 1970s. Due to the recent relaxation of planning laws in Eire, Marks & Spencer has followed an ambitious programme of opening new stores. As a Store Planner, Phil has done work in Eire on these new stores. He lives in North Nottinghamshire and regularly has to fly to Eire for work.

1   **Why do you think Marks & Spencer pays for Phil to travel to Eire rather than employ a Store Planner in that country?**
2   **Phil lives in a small village in North Nottinghamshire, which is twenty miles from Nottingham city centre and twenty miles from the centre of Doncaster in South Yorkshire. Conduct some research into which airport would be best for Phil to travel from – Nottingham East Midlands or Leeds/Bradford? Consider the cost of flights, flight times, distance from home and frequency of flights to Eire. Use this information to fully justify your answer.**
3   **The arrival of low-cost airlines has made Phil's return journeys to Eire much cheaper. Why do you think airlines such as British Midland have made many of their flights much cheaper and marketed them under the banner of bmibaby, their low-cost carrier?**
4   **Phil takes responsibility for booking the majority of his own flights. The Internet is an invaluable tool for him as he books all his flights online. Why do you think Marks & Spencer prefer him to do this rather than use their agent American Express to book tickets?**
5   **Business travellers often have very specific requirements that they wish to be met. Make a list of these requirements and suggest how airports and airlines can meet these needs.**

The nature of travel and tourism

The travel and tourism industry is continually developing to meet changing consumer needs, tastes and fashions. The characteristics of today's industry reflect its dynamic nature and the uniqueness of the products and services available.

Nature of products and services

> **Travel and tourism products and services are intangible, perishable and non-standardised**

Travel and tourism products and services take on many different forms, such as holidays, excursions and holiday insurance. All of these products have one thing in common – they are *intangible*. Imagine you are going for a haircut. Your hair is cut to the required style and length and you pay for the service. You walk out of the hairdresser's and even though you have spent money you do not actually leave the shop with anything physical in your hand. You have though enjoyed a service that has been performed for you. Holidays and other travel and tourism products and services are like this. You pay to travel on an aeroplane to a chosen destination but you do not pay to own and take away part of the aircraft. Staying in a hotel, you sleep in a bed for a night but at the end of your stay you do not take the bed away with you.

As well as being difficult to handle physically, travel and tourism products have a limited life – i.e. they are perishable. Compare a holiday to food in your fridge at home. The food in the fridge has an expiry date on it and will be no good to eat after that date. With holidays, you only stay at your destination for a given period of time and at the end of your two-week stay in Spain, for example, the holiday also expires and you have to return home.

Travel and tourism products and services are also *non-standardised*. This means that they are all different. Consider two different families. Both the Smith family and the Jones family stay in the same hotel, in the same resort on the island of Gran Canaria for the same week in July. However, the two families have two completely different holiday experiences. The Smith family are happy to lie by the pool all week soaking up the sun. The Jones family on the other hand are much happier going on excursions to see other parts of the island, para sailing and scuba diving. The same holiday booked does not mean that the whole experience will be the same for all involved and therefore standardised.

Unlike buying a car, holidays and travel and tourism products and services cannot be test driven or sampled by a customer before they decide to purchase. This is why travel and tourism products and services are presented in a glossy, colourful, highly appealing way in travel brochures, as this is often what customers are going to base their purchasing decisions on. Many holidaymakers, however, do choose to visit resorts and destinations recommended by family and friends who have already experienced the holiday and can advise from first-hand knowledge. Some

tour operators send travel agents on trips to resorts they wish to promote in order to acquire first-hand knowledge that they can use when selling tour operators' products and services. Some tour operators are finding new ways to market and promote their products and services. For example, the promotion of Disneyland Paris and Disney World in Florida can be experienced in the comfort of your own home through videos produced by the Disney corporation to encourage people to purchase holidays to its resorts.

Key terms

Intangible products These are services that have been performed for you.

Perishable products These have a limited life span.

Non-standardised products The experiences of the products vary from person to person.

There is a vast range of travel and tourism products and services to choose from, as you can see from the brochures displayed at this travel agency

For each of the travel and tourism products and services listed below, write about how they are intangible, perishable and non-standardised.

- Cruise holiday
- A city-break holiday to Prague
- Holiday insurance for a skiing trip to France
- Services supplied by a resort representative
- Car hire
- A day excursion to a traditional market in Spain, as part of a two-week holiday.

Range of products and services

The travel and tourism industry is composed of a large number of small to medium-sized enterprises whose roles are interrelated

The number of providers of travel and tourism products and services is vast. Look in your local business directory and you will see there are many organisations that can sell you a holiday, provide transportation or accommodation. Some of these organisations are part of larger regional, national or international chains, however the majority are small to medium in size and their roles are interrelated. This means that they either offer similar products and services or provide products and services that need another organisation to provide other products and services to make a customer's travel and tourism experience complete. For example, a bed and breakfast accommodation provider located near to Sherwood Forest relies on the local council properly maintaining the Sherwood Forest Country Park and the Major Oak. If these are not well looked after, then visitors will not want to come to the area and the bed and breakfast provider will experience a downturn in guest numbers.

Skills practice

This task involves researching the provision of travel and tourism products in your local area.

You need to research all the enterprises, individuals and organisations that provide tourist products and services and describe how their roles are interrelated.

Commercial organisations

The travel and tourism industry is dominated by commercial organisations

Travel and tourism organisations have many different aims and objectives. Generally they want to provide the general public with a quality service and value for money. However, the main motivation behind doing this is to make a profit. Many millions of pounds are spent each year on travel and tourism by consumers and each organisation providing the products and services wants a share of the money spent.

Commercial organisations are those that operate to make a profit and are therefore in the private sector of the economy. The private sector of the economy is made up of organisations that are started by entrepreneurs, individuals or groups. The government provides no resources to this sector of the economy.

The main purpose of commercial organisations is to make a profit

Many of the largest companies in the UK are involved in travel and tourism. Examples include British Airways, Forte (hotels) and the Tussaud's Group that owns attractions including Madame Tussaud's and Alton Towers.

* REMEMBER!

The main aim of commercial organisations is to make a profit.

Think about it

Why do you think the travel and tourism industry is dominated by commercial organisations?

Public and voluntary organisations

The travel and tourism industry is supported and influenced by public and voluntary organisations

Commercial organisations may dominate the travel and tourism industry, however both the public and voluntary sectors of the economy play a role in supporting and influencing the industry.

Public sector facilities are funded and controlled by the government. This could be national government or local government, such as local councils. The government has become involved in tourism because of the positive effects of tourism and the income and jobs that are created by the industry.

Voluntary sector organisations are funded and run by volunteer organisations. Most of their income comes from membership fees, gifts, legacies, selling merchandise and public appeals. Organisations in the public or voluntary sectors do not aim to make a profit; they merely provide services and support the industry. So, how do these two sectors support and influence the travel and tourism industry?

Public sector organisations involved in travel in tourism include the British Tourist Authority (BTA), the English Tourism Council (ETC), the Wales Tourist Board (WTB) and the Scottish Tourist Board (STB). These organisations are funded by central government (national government) and in 1999–2000 the Department for Culture, Media and Sport gave just under £50 million to the BTA and ETC. The STB and WTB both received over £15 million each from their own executives. Services provided by these tourism authorities include providing tourist information offices, funding marketing campaigns and funding new tourism facilities. They also play an advisory role in helping principals in the private sector to make decisions and respond to current trends and fashions by providing information on visitor numbers, for example.

One way in which the public sector has worked to support tourism is by scrapping admission fees to many of London's top museums and attractions. In the year 2003–2004, visitor numbers to these attractions were thought to have increased by around 50 per cent.

Think about it

Why do you think the government would want to subsidise attractions such as the British Museum and the National History Museum in London?

Voluntary organisations in the travel and tourism industry are generally formed to

* meet a particular interest or need in the community, for example a sport

* raise interest in a particular problem, such as a conservation issue

* encourage constructive use of leisure time, for example Scouts and Guides.

The National Trust is probably the most important voluntary sector organisation involved in tourism. Its work ranges from protecting historic buildings, gardens and coastlines, which attract millions of visitors a year. In recent years, the organisation has also run conservation holidays for volunteers who want to do something useful with their leisure time. Activities for volunteers can range from conducting wildlife surveys to laying new hedgerows. The National Trust runs working holidays called Acorn Projects and Oak Camps. The Royal Society for the Protection of Birds (RSPB) also offers holidays in its reserves for volunteers who want to do conservation work.

The National Trust offers holiday facilities such as accommodation and attractions such as historic buildings

Skills practice

Visit a local National Trust attraction. Take a tour of the attraction to get a sense of the work undertaken by the organisation. Try to find out information on visitor numbers.

Think about it

What contribution do you think voluntary sector organisations make to the tourism industry?

Very often organisations in the private, public and voluntary sectors work together, for example on conserving and maintaining tourist attractions.

Key terms

Private sector This comprises those organisations that operate to make a profit.
Public sector This comprises those organisations that are funded and controlled by government.
Voluntary sector This comprises those organisations that are funded and run by volunteer agencies.

Think about it

How do you think organisations in the private, public and voluntary sectors can work together?

Internal and external pressures

The travel and tourism industry is vulnerable to internal and external pressures

What stops you doing what you want to do? Is it that you don't have enough money to go on a dream holiday or do your parents insist that you are back home by a certain time in the evenings? Or was the concert you had booked tickets for months in advance cancelled because the lead singer of the band was ill? Some of these effects on your life are *internal* and can be controlled to a certain degree by yourself. Other effects are *external* and you have no control over these. The travel and tourism industry is no different as it is also vulnerable to internal and external pressures.

Examples of the internal pressures on the travel and tourism industry are health and safety issues and the need to rationalise costs.

Think about it

What other internal pressures do you think organisations in the travel and tourism industry are under?

External pressures are more difficult to control. Even though organisations can plan to deal with

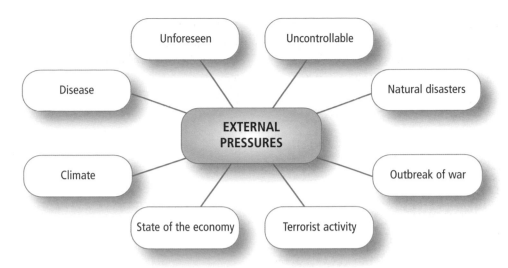

Figure 1.4 External pressures are more difficult to control than internal pressures

these pressures, the responses to them are primarily reactionary in nature.

The principals of the travel and tourism industry (the different organisations who offer different products and services) must find ways to deal with both internal and external pressures to minimise their impact on operations and revenues/profits.

Recent pressures on the travel and tourism industry have mainly been external in their nature. Examples that have had a huge impact on the travel and tourism industry include the 9/11 attacks on New York, the SARS virus, the Iraq conflict and the South East Asian tsunami.

Skills practice

In 2001, an outbreak of Foot and Mouth disease swept across the UK. Carry out research to answer the following questions.

1 What is Foot and Mouth disease and whom does it affect?
2 Which areas of the UK were most affected by the outbreak of the disease?
3 What measures were put in place to reduce the spread of the disease?
4 How do you think the outbreak of the disease affected the UK tourism industry? Consider the impact on both domestic and inbound tourism.

CASE STUDY

9/11

A day that shook the world – September 11th 2002. This was the day terrorists hijacked passenger aircraft and flew them into the Twin Towers buildings of the World Trade Organisation in New York. These huge, impressive buildings crumbled to the ground and thousands of people lost their lives.

1 **What impact do you think this tragic event had on travel and tourism?**
2 **Why do you think the numbers of people travelling globally, not just in America, declined after this event?**
3 **As a result of 9/11, security in airports the world over has been stepped up to try and prevent another tragedy such as this. What do you think have been the consequences of improved and heightened security measures for ordinary travellers?**
4 **What do you think are the challenges facing tourism officials in America in the aftermath of this event?**

CASE STUDY

Tsunami sweeps South East Asia

Boxing Day 2004, thousands of tourists were waking to another day in paradise. The beaches of South East Asia were beginning to fill with holidaymakers ready to soak up the sunshine of a glorious day. Resorts in Thailand, Indonesia, India and Sri Lanka were busy and full of European tourists escaping the traditional cold weather of the festive period in Europe.

At around 9.30 in the morning local time, the unthinkable happened. An underwater earthquake measuring approximately 9 on the Richter scale, the world's fourth worst earthquake since records began, shook the area without warning and created gigantic tidal waves which pounded coastal areas in the region. Whole towns and resorts were destroyed, hundreds of thousands lost their lives, disease became a real threat and supplies of fresh water and food ran out.

The rest of the world launched massive relief projects to help the people and local economies of those areas affected. Tourists who were left with little more than the clothes they had on were flown home, whilst others continued their holidays.

1   Tourism has played a major part in supporting the economies of less economically developed countries in South East Asia. What impact do you think the tsunami will have had on tourism in the area?

2   As a tourism official in one of the affected countries, how would you try to attract visitors back to the area?

3   Those tourists who survived unscathed from the tsunami and continued with their holidays were criticised in the media for enjoying themselves sunbathing and drinking in the midst of such tragedy. Do you think the tourism authorities in affected countries would have been pleased that tourists behaved in this way? Explain your answer.

4   Natural disasters happen all over the world. Can you think of any other tourist destinations that have been hit by a natural disaster in recent years?

An example of the devastation caused by the tsunami that struck coastal resort areas of South East Asia on Boxing Day 2004

The economic climate in a country also has an impact on tourism. Economies behave in a cyclical fashion. At times economies and countries are prosperous, with the majority of people in work earning money and spending that money. The opposite of this boom situation is a recession. If a country's economy is in recession, then unemployment is high and people have less money to spend on luxuries and non-necessities such as travel and tourism.

> **Think about it**
>
> How would you describe the term 'economy'?

> **Key terms**
>
> **Internal pressure** This is pressure that can be controlled to some extent by you.
>
> **External pressure** This is pressure you cannot control.

Impact of travel and tourism

> **Travel and tourism activities impact on destinations and host communities**

Governments across the world are keen to promote and support tourism, as the industry is a major provider of foreign investment and jobs. However, not all the impacts of tourism on host destinations and communities are seen as positive. Both the positive and negative impacts of tourism is examined below in terms of their effects on the economy, culture and environment of host communities. *Host communities* are the people who live in the areas that tourists visit.

Positive economic impacts of tourism

* Job creation – employees are needed to work in hotels, restaurants and other facilities aimed at attracting tourists.
* Wealth creation – local people employed in the travel and tourism industry earn money and in turn demand and consume more products and services. This has an impact on jobs in other industries.
* Other parts of the world become aware of the host destination and community, and so trade other than tourism may result from this.
* The infrastructure of an area is improved. Roads and airports are built to deal with the increased number of visitors, again increasing job and earning opportunities.
* Tourists spend money on food and drink, accommodation and entertainment. This money is spent at local businesses and some of this is then invested in providing new facilities that locals as well as tourists can use and enjoy.

Negative economic impacts of tourism

* Prices of goods, services and houses tend to rise in tourist areas. These prices often rise too high for the people of the host communities to afford.
* Seasonal work. Many jobs that are created by the tourism industry are only temporary, so local workers may have reduced incomes during the 'off-season', when no or fewer tourists visit.
* Tourism depends on other economies flourishing. For example, if lots of German tourists visit a particular resort each year, and then the German economy goes into recession with increases in taxation, interest rates and unemployment, this may mean that many Germans can no longer afford to holiday at the resort.
* Loss of local services. Shops may become more geared towards serving tourists than locals, with, for example, the sale of souvenirs taking over from the sale of groceries.
* Jobs in tourism are notoriously low paid.
* Many hotels are owned by companies based in other countries. The profits from these hotels therefore do not stay in the host community but flow out to another country. This has an impact on future development of the area.

Positive cultural impacts of tourism

✱ Host communities have contact with the outside world and the people become more educated, for example learning other languages to be able to communicate with tourists.

✱ As facilities increase, the social life of the population increases.

✱ Rather than dying out with older generations, cultures and traditions can be preserved and remembered because tourists find them interesting.

Negative cultural impacts of tourists

✱ Loss of identity. Host communities can feel like strangers as the tourists take over.

✱ Bad habits and practices can be spread, for example tourists introduce smoking, drinking and recreational drug-taking that host communities may not have been exposed to before.

✱ Traditions and religions can become ignored because tourists have no knowledge of them.

✱ Host communities can be exploited by tourists.

Positive environmental impacts of tourism

✱ Derelict and run-down areas are cleaned up and regenerated.

✱ Old buildings are converted into tourist accommodation.

✱ Areas are pedestrianised and signposting is improved.

Negative environmental impacts of tourism

✱ Physical erosion of landscapes and coastlines.

✱ Litter.

✱ Increased pollution – air, sea and noise pollution.

✱ Increased traffic congestion.

✱ Disturbance of wildlife.

✱ Reduction of natural habitats.

✱ Alteration of landscapes.

✱ Encouragment of inappropriate development.

Skills practice

Tourism is a developing industry in many countries, particularly as travellers want to visit more exotic locations. You are to write a project on the impact of tourism on either The Gambia or Phuket in Thailand. Your project should have the following structure:

• Where the destination is located and what facilities it has

• Economic impacts on host communities of tourism (positive and negative)

• Cultural impacts on host communities of tourism (positive and negative)

• Environmental impacts on host communities of tourism (positive and negative)

• Evaluation – overall do you think tourism has benefited or hindered the destination you have investigated?

Think about it

How can tourist destinations work to reduce the negative impacts of tourism?

Moves have been made in recent years to take a more responsible attitude towards tourism, especially where it is a growing industry in the less economically developed countries. The aim has been to protect host communities from being exploited and to reduce the impact of pollution on natural environments.

Key terms associated with this movement are *responsible tourism*, *sustainable tourism* and *eco-tourism*. *Responsible tourism* refers not only to developers taking a sensible approach towards the development of tourist resorts but also to the way in which tourists behave and the activities they take part in whilst in a resort. For example, responsible tourism can include the choice of souvenirs that tourists choose to purchase. An example of this is tourists to Africa not buying souvenirs made from ivory and therefore not supporting the illegal trade of elephant hunting and ivory poaching.

Sustainable tourism seeks to tackle the long-term environmental and social issues surrounding uncontrolled tourism development. Much development in tourist destinations has taken place on an ad hoc basis and has become disjointed because there has been little formal planning and control. Sustainable tourism aims to strike a healthy balance between conserving areas of natural beauty, meeting the needs of local people and the desire to attract tourists and meet their demands.

Skills practice

New Zealand, a country of many contrasts, has worked hard to develop its tourism industry whilst retaining the natural beauty of the country. Conduct research to find out how New Zealand has tried to develop an ethos of sustainable tourism.

The natural beauty of New Zealand is one of the great attractions for tourists

Green issues and the environment have become important issues in the travel and tourism industry. Global warming and climate change have been at the centre of many concerns and *eco-tourism* is an ethos that promotes environmentally friendly tourism. This involves resorts and accommodation being built out of locally sourced materials that are also replenishable. Some resorts in Indonesia have been built using such materials and are also powered by solar power.

Key terms

Responsible tourism The development of resorts and the behaviour of tourists that do not produce undesirable effects.

Sustainable tourism This is the balance between conserving areas and meeting local needs and attracting tourists and meeting their demands.

Eco-tourism This promotes environmentally friendly tourism.

Think about it

The Lake District is an area of outstanding natural beauty in the UK. What can you suggest that allows tourism in this area to continue to grow and develop but at the same time protect the environment?

Think about it

In your own words define the following:
- Responsible tourism
- Sustainable tourism
- Eco-tourism.

The development of the travel and tourism industry

To help you understand the nature of today's travel and tourism industry, it is important that you realise how the industry has developed over a long period of time. This section will examine the historical developments and factors that have contributed to creating the dynamic, ever-changing and still-developing travel and tourism industry of today.

In this section you will learn:

* The factors contributing to the emergence of mass tourism, rather than tourism for the wealthy elite

* The technological developments relating to infrastructure, transport and information systems and their impact on tourism destinations

* The product development, innovation and the major developments which have shaped the industry

* The needs of consumers, their expectations and fashions change, and organisations in the travel and tourism industry must respond to these changes.

Tourism for all?

One hundred and fifty years ago holidays were a luxury only the wealthy could afford to enjoy. The UK seaside resorts, for example, were once the

In Victorian times only those who were rich enough could afford to take holidays

preserve of rich Victorians who took the sea air as part of their health regimes. So how has the travel and tourism industry developed so that the majority of people now participate in travel and tourism activities in some way?

There are various factors that explain the emergence of the mass tourism. These include:

* Socio-economic influences
* Technological developments
* Product development and innovation
* Changing consumer needs, expectations and fashions.

The development of the travel and tourism industry has taken place over many years and the growth of leisure travel has its origins in the nineteenth century.

Travel and tourism in the nineteenth century

Finding a cure for medical ailments led to the introduction of holiday centres in the eighteenth century. For the wealthy who could afford to travel and who also had time for cures to take effect, the spa towns of Bath, Scarborough and Cheltenham, and coastal towns such as Brighton and Bognor Regis, became popular. The wealthy who visited these resorts believed that taking to the waters would cure a range of illnesses and conditions, from rheumatism to gout. As the number of visitors to these resorts increased, the demand for entertainment and accommodation grew. At this time overseas travel was the

preserve of the aristocracy and those who were extremely well-connected and wealthy. Young aristocrats were often sent on a 'Grand Tour' of European cities as this was believed to be a valuable part of their education.

It was not until the emergence of the railways in the nineteenth century that the less wealthy began to enjoy visiting seaside resorts. Resorts such as Margate, Blackpool and Southport grew as a result of direct transport links with major cities. People also travelled to the resorts by road, often by stagecoach, but this was slower than travelling by rail and was more expensive. Hotels were built close to many of the new railway stations to service the growing demand for travel and accommodation.

As well as developments in transportation, the nineteenth century saw a shift in the geographical distribution of people from rural locations to new urban areas. As workers moved from the countryside as a result of the Industrial Revolution to take jobs in the new mills and factories, the earning potential of this group increased. This in turn meant that more people had disposable income to spend on leisure pursuits, transport and travel. However, only a minority of people could afford to access travel and transportation; the majority of the population were still excluded by the cost.

Overseas travel also became increasingly popular during the latter half of the nineteenth century. The Great Exhibition at Crystal Palace in 1851, for example, attracted visitors from all parts of the British Empire.

Carry out research using your library to help you answer the following questions.

1 What was the Great Exhibition of 1851?

2 Who organised the Great Exhibition?

3 What effect do you think the Great Exhibition had on tourism in the UK?

Travel and tourism in the twentieth century

During the twentieth century, the travel and tourism industry grew rapidly into the industry it is today. For socio-economic and technological reasons, many more people were able to participate in travel and tourism activities and this developed into mass tourism.

Pollution, congestion, and parking difficulties are common problems we face with modern motoring and the use of cars. However, this has not always been the case. At the beginning of the twentieth century, car ownership was restricted to the wealthy few and cars were not viewed as the reliable mode of transport they are today. During the inter-war years (1919–1938), car ownership grew as cars were manufactured more cheaply and prices fell. New tourist areas were opened up, particularly those that had previously been inaccessible by ferry or train. With improved road networks, more restaurants, hotels and caravan sites emerged as travellers could go further than ever before. Bus and coach companies also flourished as travellers became more adventurous and paid holidays gave the working classes the opportunity to take time off work and afford to spend a holiday away from home, even if only for a week.

Before travel to overseas destinations became popular with UK tourists from the 1950s onwards, most people would holiday in the UK, particularly in holiday resorts such as Butlins and Pontin's, which became popular for family holidays. The resorts (which were called 'camps' at the time) provided all the necessary facilities on site and they could be accessed from any part of the country by way of the extensive network of dual carriageways and major roads that had been built.

The development of the travel and tourism industry is a key component of Unit 1 for the Applied GCE in Travel and Tourism. The external examination requires you to be able to write confidently about some of the major developments in the industry, such as the creation of holiday resorts in the UK, which was a major turning point in the working classes accessing holidays and becoming tourists. The following activity will not only help to improve your research skills but will help in building your knowledge for your examination.

Conduct as much research as you can on Billy Butlin, the man who founded Butlins' holiday resorts, and create a report using the following as headings to guide your research. Your report should be in a formal business style.

1 How it all began – the first holiday resort, Skegness 1937

2 The growth of the holiday resorts

3 Competitors to Butlins

4 The 1970s and 1980s – why did visitor numbers to holiday centres fall?

5 The 1990s – making holiday resorts attractive again

6 Now and the future – what is on offer at the holiday resorts today and what does the future hold?

A modern Butlins holiday resort

Holiday resorts such as Butlins and Pontin's enjoyed great popularity; some employers even developed resorts just for their own staff to visit and use. The civil service was one example, where the idea was to provide employees with subsidised holidays to keep them motivated, as it was believed that staff who played together would also work much better together!

As travel by road became increasingly popular, fewer people were travelling by sea and rail than in the nineteenth century. Car ownership and the technological innovations in the air travel industry meant that travel by road and air became the preferred methods of transport by most travellers by the end of the twentieth century.

The development of fighting airforces in the First and Second World Wars paved the way for much of the development in the air travel industry. The advances made in knowledge and technology was transferred to commercial airlines, so that by 1952 travellers were being transported from the UK to the other side of the world using new turbojet technology. Air travel was twice as fast at the end of the Second World War as it had been at the beginning. The need for trained pilots during the war meant that after the end of hostilities, many men were qualified to fly and were employed by the new and emerging commercial passenger airlines.

CASE STUDY

Growing up on a holiday camp

Paul is now in his fifties, but recounts growing up on a holiday camp run by the civil service for their staff. His parents worked in the holiday camp.

'We lived in a cottage tied to the holiday camp. It was quite primitive really – no mains electricity, no running water and no indoor loo. It was really bleak and a far cry from the holiday camp where civil service staff would come in the summer for their one or two week holiday.

'The holiday camp was just outside Scarborough in Yorkshire and my parents had moved from London to Scarborough to find work there. Dad worked as a chef and Mum as a cleaner. I'm not sure how good a chef Dad was, but he got the job as he'd been in the army catering corps during the war. Mum cleaned out the chalets, which were like rows of Nissan huts and I suppose they were quite simple inside. I have photographs of my parents with the rest of the camp's staff from each year they worked there. Dad looked all smart in his chef's whites, Mum had a tunic-type uniform and the staff who ran all the sporting activities for guests wore crisp white uniforms and looked quite fearsome!

'As a child I was allowed free roam of the holiday camp during the school summer holidays. I would help out and watch all the different activities. The holidays were really hectic, with guests running from one activity or contest to the next. It didn't seem very relaxing to me! Meal times were always fascinating to watch. Guests queued up to take their seats in the large restaurant and would be called up table by table to help themselves from the buffet. It was more like a work's canteen actually, but the food always smelt good and there never seemed to be any left. Perhaps Dad was an okay cook after all!

'We left the holiday camp when Dad went to work for the local water board. I still remember it well though'

1 Do you think that today's tourists would enjoy staying at a holiday camp like the one described in the case study? Explain your answer.
2 Why do you think employers who ran such holiday camps closed them down in the 1960s and 1970s?

The UK holiday resorts were able to provide all the entertainment, food and other facilities for a family holiday, however there was one thing they couldn't guarantee – good summer holiday weather. So the idea of taking holidays overseas where the weather was guaranteed to be dry, hot and sunny had considerable appeal to the British holidaymaker; and the package holiday was born.

The British were soon flocking to the Spanish Mediterranean resorts of Benidorm, Lloret de Mar and Torremolinos on package holidays. Spain offered great weather, another culture and cheap food and wine. Costa Brava, Costa Dorada, Costa del Sol and Costa Blanca also became popular with UK tourists, and early holidaymakers to these resorts paid as little as £50 for their holiday in paradise. As package holidaymakers became more adventurous, they began travelling to Portugal, Greece and Turkey, for example.

CASE STUDY

Marjorie and George

Marjorie and George live in Derby and go on holiday at least three times a year to an overseas destination. Their favourite destinations include Benidorm in Spain, Santa Ponsa on the Spanish island of Majorca and Playa de las Americas on the island of Tenerife. They first started visiting Mediterranean resorts in the early 1960s and discuss some of their experiences here.

Marjorie: Before we started going to Spain, we would visit UK seaside resorts such as Skegness, Bridlington and Blackpool. I really liked those places, they were good fun.

George: If what you describe as running from one bus shelter to the next and from café to café to avoid the rain as fun, then I suppose it was. I remember going to Skegness one year and it rained so much that the caravan we were staying in sank in the field. We left the caravan only a handful of times during the week we were there.

Marjorie: That's why we first started going abroad. One of George's friends from work had been to Spain the same week we spent in the caravan at Skegness. They came back all nice and brown and we came back soggy! I said to George that I'd love to feel the sunshine on my face and Spain seemed so exotic.

George: I agreed to go and we've never looked back since. We went to Benidorm the first time and stayed in a lovely, brand-new hotel. It was all shiny marble and white and clean and absolutely nothing like our old caravan. I was sold. No more summers in the rain in caravans or guesthouses where you have to be out all-day and back in at 11 at night.

Marjorie: The freedom was great. The weather was great. And most of all the wine was great. It was all so different from going on holiday at home. We saw flamenco dancers at night, sat on the beach during the day and ate in the hotel three times a day. Our neighbours were so jealous when we returned and everyone wanted to see our photos.

George: And we got to fly, so no driving for me. Even now, it's Spain every time for us when we go on holiday.

1   Why do you think Mediterranean resorts became centres for mass tourism?
2   When Mediterranean resorts first became popular what do you think was the impact on British resorts?
3   Not everybody likes to go overseas for his or her holidays. Why do you think some tourists prefer to holiday at home?
4   Many resorts in the UK have to compete with overseas resorts for holidaymakers. Imagine you work for a local tourist board and want to attract tourists to your area. How could you do this?

Travel to overseas destinations meant that UK residents were spending their money abroad and not in this country. This, coupled with a decline in visitor numbers to UK destinations, led to the Development of Tourism Act of 1969. Tourism potentially earned the country a great deal of money and provided many jobs. Around the world economies were growing and booming as most of the world recovered from the struggle of the post-war years. People were more inquisitive and wanted to travel and explore, so the 1969 Act aimed to coordinate marketing activities of promoting the UK as a holiday destination to foreigners and to improve facilities that would attract tourists. Regional tourist boards were also established to help promote tourism in particular areas of the UK.

Skills practice

Contact your local tourist board to find out about the range of activities they are involved in to promote your area as a tourist attraction.

Throughout the twentieth century, travel and tourism continued to evolve and to provide a host of products and services tourists could choose from. From the introduction of holiday camps to the emergence of the package holiday to overseas destinations, tourism was certainly very different at the end of the century than at the beginning. Consumer needs have changed dramatically and the choice of holidays is wide-ranging, including beach holidays, long-haul destinations, activity holidays, short breaks, self-drives and fly-drives.

Travel and tourism in the twenty-first century

Technology and the sophistication of modern tourists have ensured that already in this century the travel and tourism industry has seen many changes.

The growth in the use of personal computers has had a huge impact on the travel and tourism industry and poses a threat to many of the traditional principals involved in servicing customers. Product development and innovation has played a large role in the changing face of the industry. Internet travel companies such as lastminute.com and ebookers enable tourists to become more independent and avoid the services of a travel agent. Package holidays are still popular but there has been considerable growth in the cruise sector. This sector was previously seen as catering for the older generation but now taking a cruise is seen as being in a 'floating hotel', with all amenities under one roof and providing the opportunity to visit different destinations.

Developments in travel and tourism

The brief history of the development of the travel and tourism industry has given an insight into how the industry has reached its current position. Tourism and travel provide in the region of two million jobs in the UK and more than 25 million overseas visitors are attracted to the UK each year. The industry is of utmost importance to the UK economy. Some of the main historical developments and factors that have led to the growth of the industry and its current characteristics will now be examined in more detail.

Changes in socio-economic circumstances

We have already seen that over the last two centuries travel and tourism has become more accessible to the working classes. Traditionally, only the wealthy could afford to travel, so how have the working classes been able to increasingly participate in travel and tourism?

Better pay and conditions for workers is the key to why more people could afford to travel and spend a holiday away from home. Legislation compelled employers to treat their workers better and in 1938 the government passed the Holidays with Pay Act. This increased the potential for holidaymaking among workers. Previously holidays were unpaid or unauthorised, which meant that workers would either lose money or their jobs. However, the 1938 Act was not strictly observed until a decade after it was introduced, and it was then that people's travel behaviour really began to change.

Paid holidays, as well as reduced working hours, gave workers more leisure time and more disposable income. Disposable income is what you have left to spend after all of your bills and overheads have been paid. Having more money enabled the working classes to take daytrips, buy cars and go on holidays. So, the changes in their socio-economic circumstances enabled the working classes to take part in tourist activities.

Technological developments

Technology has played a major role in the growth of the travel and tourism industry. In particular, the development of transport systems and infrastructure has allowed visitors to access previously inaccessible destinations. The introduction of the railways, passenger ferries, cars and aeroplanes has enabled people to travel, and without them travel tourism would not exist.

As well as the building of railway tracks and stations, motorways and airports, the development of new materials offering greater flexibility, durability and strength has affected the design of aeroplanes, cars and communication systems, making them cheaper and longer lasting. These costs are then in turn passed on to customers.

The use of computers has revolutionised many aspects of the travel and tourism industry. Notable examples include air traffic control, automated aircraft flying and landing procedures, computerised navigation, automated baggage handling, hotel management and security systems and payment systems.

Think about it

Computers have changed the face of the travel industry. What would happen if computerised air traffic control systems failed?

Skills practice

Recently a new national air traffic control centre was opened in the UK. You need to conduct research to find out the name of the new centre and to find out about some of the problems encountered in opening such an expensive and crucial system.

Booking holidays has become easier due to advances in technology. Travel arrangements can now be made much more quickly and easily through central reservation systems which travel agents can access. These central reservation systems allow the travel agent to book, confirm and issue tickets instantly and whilst the customer is in the shop. Walk into almost any travel agent and each sales consultant will be equipped with a personal computer on their desk that allows them to access information from a range of tour operators. The central reservation systems hold banks of information about available holidays, scheduled airline bookings, car rental, hotel accommodation and the booking of excursions, activities and other entertainments. A queuing system is used to manage incoming messages and requests for travel arrangements and a customer's details can be saved and held ready for when they wish to make a reservation. Tour operators are also able to respond quickly to unsold holidays by offering special deals and promotions to travel agents, and ultimately to customers.

Computers have revolutionised the travel and tourism industry, particularly in air traffic control

You are a sales consultant in a branch of one of the country's most successful chains of travel agents. What are the advantages and disadvantages of using computerised central reservation systems?

Product development, innovation and changing consumer needs

The range of products and services offered to customers has become increasingly sophisticated, a long way from the early days of excursions offered by Thomas Cook. Through any travel agent you can book a holiday and you can purchase insurance, organise car rental and book airport car parking.

Tourists have also become more sophisticated and knowledgeable, and therefore more demanding in what they want. They look for new places to visit and better offers from travel and tourism organisations. Those organisations which fail to meet these sorts of demands risk going out of business. The following are examples of product development and innovation over time:

* Thomas Cook's first overseas tour to the USA in 1855

* Billy Butlin opens his first holiday resort in 1937

* Package holidays introduced to the Mediterranean in the 1950s and 1960s

* Growth of budget airlines offering customers cheap flights to a range of destinations in the 1990s

* Growth of the cruising sector and the cruise ship as 'floating hotel' in the early 2000s.

Not only have the products changed dramatically over the years, so have the ways you can buy these products. Thomas Cook pioneered the idea of travel agents operating from an office through which customers can make their travel arrangements. Some tour operators then decided to cut out the 'middle man' and sell their holidays direct to the general public. People could then book holidays by filling out and sending off an order form or by using the telephone to contact the tour operator. Other tour operators use new technologies to promote and sell holidays, for example on television information systems such as Teletext and through advertising on commercial television channels. Viewers can browse through hundreds of offers and then telephone tour operators to take advantage of the offers. In recent years the growth of satellite and cable television channels has stimulated the setting up of channels dedicated to informing viewers about particular holiday destinations and selling a variety of holidays to them.

Television is a powerful medium for advertising and selling holidays. However, the Internet has made the greatest impact on the travel and tourism industry in recent times. There are many websites selling holidays to travellers who are increasingly confident about making their own travel arrangements. Lastminute.com and ebookers are well-established websites that bring together different elements of the travel and tourism industry and often have special offers saving tourists lots of money.

Visit the websites of three Internet travel companies.

1 For each of the websites you visit, create a list of the products and services offered by that Internet travel company.

2 Evaluate each of the websites in terms of
   • ease of use/navigation
   • layout
   • number of destinations offered
   • number of special offers/savings that can be made.

3 Which, in your opinion, offers the best products and services to customers? Explain your answer fully.

4 What are the weaknesses, if there are any, of the websites you visited?

5 How would you improve the services offered by Internet travel companies?

6 Why do you think Internet travel companies have become so popular?

7 What impact do you think these Internet travel companies have had on traditional travel and tourism companies?

ICT has played a major role in changing the travel and tourism industry. Another major influence has been the changing requirements of customers. Tourists have become more sophisticated and demanding in their needs, with the result that destinations and resorts fall in and out of fashion as tourists satisfy those needs. Early travel companies offered customers only a narrow range of holidays, so in that sense they dictated what kind of holidays people had. However, tourists are now much more sophisticated and through what they demand from a holiday they dictate what the travel companies must be prepared to offer. Travel companies must now follow fashions and the requirements of customers if they are to stay trading.

The Mediterranean resorts became so popular in the 1960s because of the way they were marketed to people, the majority of whom had never been overseas before. At the time these resorts were perceived as exotic, however as tourists became more knowledgeable about the destinations and confident about travelling to holiday at these, they began demanding different holiday destinations, so that in the 1980s and 1990s holiday fashions moved from the Mediterranean to Greece, America, the Caribbean and the Far East.

The needs of consumers have changed and they now expect so much more from their travels. They now demand many different types of holidays. Examples include:

* Short-breaks to city destinations
* Long-haul holidays to exotic destinations
* Activity holidays – skiing, cycling, painting
* Self-drive
* Fly-drive
* Self-packaging (independently booking and organising holidays without the help of travel agents).

Skills practice

For your external examination, you need to study at least two destinations in the UK and overseas. In preparation for the examination, the next activity will provide you with case studies that you can then use in your examination answers.

CASE STUDY

Benidorm

Changing consumer needs, expectations and fashions have had a significant influence on the travel and tourism industry. Benidorm in Spain has long been a favourite of British holidaymakers and it is your task to conduct research on this Mediterranean resort. Once you have collected research to answer the questions below, you will be able to make judgements about the success of the resort using your skills of analysis and evaluation.

1 **Whereabouts in Spain is Benidorm located? Which airport serves the resort? How far away are any of Spain's large cities?**
2 **How did Benidorm grow into the resort it is today? (This needs to include information about the historical development of the resort.)**
3 **When and why did Benidorm become so popular with British tourists?**
4 **What attractions and facilities does Benidorm have today to attract tourists?**
5 **How many British tourists visit Benidorm each year?**
6 **Is Benidorm as popular today as it once was? Why?**
7 **What threats are there to Benidorm continuing as a holiday hotspot?**
8 **How can the resort respond to any threats and changes in consumer demands?**

As another case study of an overseas resort, this task can be repeated for Florida or for the resort of Kardamena on the Greek island of Kos.

The following are the milestones in the development of travel and tourism.

1700s	Paid employment and regulated working hours
1750s	Beginning of the Industrial Revolution
1815	First steam-driven sea voyage (Glasgow to Dublin)
1830	First passenger train service (Manchester to Liverpool)
1840s	Cunard began a regular shipping service to America. P & O sailed regularly to India and the Far East
1841	Thomas Cook's first 'day' excursion from Leicester to Loughborough via rail
1851	The Great Exhibition at Crystal Palace attracts visitors from far and wide
1855	Thomas Cook organises his first overseas tour to the Paris Exhibition of 1855
1860	Invention of bicycle – independent travel for the masses
1860s	Regular ferry services to Ireland and across the Channel were in operation
1865	Thomas Cook opens an office in London
1866	Thomas Cook organises first tour to America
1869	The opening of the Suez Canal makes India and the Far East easier to travel to
1869	The USA could be completely crossed by rail as a link between the Union Pacific and Central Pacific railways is opened
1870	60-hour working week became the standard. Half-day holiday introduced on Saturday afternoon, later known as the weekend
1871	Bank Holiday Act establishes four public Bank Holidays
1880s	The first skiing holidaymakers travelled from the UK to Switzerland
1885	Invention of the motorcar
1900s	Vast improvement in road, rail, sea and air transport
1918	After the First World War, bus and coach services began to appear

1920s	Air services develop mainly to transport mail to the British colonies and to carry military personnel. Air travel is still expensive and unreliable at this time
1935	Approximately 500,000 visitors crowded into Brighton on August Bank Holiday. The majority arrived by rail or specially organised coach services
1935	Gatwick aerodrome opened to relieve congestion at Croydon. At this time Gatwick could handle six aircraft at a time
1936	First train ferry service between Dover and Dunkirk. Passengers would leave London Victoria station at 10 pm and arrive in France at 8.55 am, the next day
1937	The first Butlins holiday resort is opened in Skegness
1938	Holidays with Pay Act
1939	First transatlantic passenger flight
1940s	London's main air terminal transferred from Croydon to Heathrow. British airlines include British Overseas Airways Corporation (BOAC) and British European Airways (BEA)
1945	After the Second World War, there was a dramatic increase in air travel due to the number of trained pilots available
1950s	Construction and opening of the motorway network is under way
1950	First package holiday organised by Horizon to Corsica. Other tour operators quickly organised packages to other Mediterranean resorts
1952	First jet airline passenger service from London to Johannesburg
1960s	Introduction of 37-hour working week
1968	First cross-Channel hovercraft service
1969	The Development of Tourism Act sees the establishment of tourist boards, showing the government's recognition of tourism as an income generator and as an employer
1970	Travel allowance charged by the government for people wishing to travel overseas is abolished

1970	First Boeing 747 carries 352 on a transatlantic flight
1971	BOAC and BEA merge and are administered by the British Airways Board
1974	Clarksons, a major holiday company, goes out of business, stranding 50,000 tourists abroad. Issues highlighted include the structure of pricing for holidays and consumer protection
1976	Concorde goes into service
1977	Laker Airways is established to challenge major national airlines with cheaper transatlantic air tickets
1978	Spending by British holidaymakers overseas exceeds their spending on domestic tourism for the first time
1980	The International Leisure Group starts to offer cheap package holidays to Florida
1982	Laker Airways goes out of business
1990s	Eurotunnel carries first passengers
1991	The International Leisure Group, which had organised cheap package holidays to Florida, go out of business due to the Gulf War and recession in the UK
1991	A national marketing campaign, 'Discover the English Seaside', was launched in an attempt to arrest the decline of traditional UK seaside resorts
1992	The number of foreign visitors to the UK grows to 18.5 million
1992	Euro-Disney (later known as Disneyland Paris) is opened
1995	More people are finding out about the Internet and more people start to travel independently, organising travel and accommodation online
2000s	Low-cost airlines offering reduced price tickets to a number of European destinations are established and become very popular with a new breed of independent travellers. Examples include easyJet, Ryanair, Go and bmibaby
2003	Concorde decommissioned from service

A television producer has approached you about a new television series for the Applied GCE in Travel and Tourism. The aim of the television series is to cover the main units of the qualification and each thirty-minute programme is to feature a different unit. For Unit 1, Inside Travel and Tourism, you have been asked to write a script for the development of the tourism section of the first programme. Use the following brief to help write your script:

- Your script should be in the form of a documentary – therefore it should be informative and authoritative.

- You have a five-minute slot in the programme.

- You need to include information on travel and tourism in the nineteenth century, travel and tourism in the twentieth century, reasons for developments in the industry and the future of the industry.

Different sectors of the travel and tourism industry

As we have already examined in earlier sections the travel and tourism industry is large, forever changing and consists of many organisations. These organisations range in size from individual to multinational companies. Most of them are commercial and therefore in the private sector. Some, such as tourist information offices, may be funded by local and/or national government and are in the public sector. A small number are run by charities. These organisations are usually interested in sustainable tourism and help to protect host destinations from exploitation and pollution.

Organisations in the travel and tourism industry can be grouped into different sectors depending on the types of products and services they offer.

In this section you will learn about:

* The different sectors of the industry

* The types of organisation within each sector of the industry

* The role of organisations within each sector.

Each sector of the travel and tourism industry will be investigated in turn.

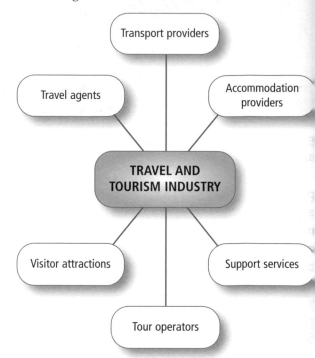

Figure 1.5 Sectors of the travel and tourism indust[ry]

Transport providers

This is concerned with the range of travel options available to independent tourists, package holidaymakers and business travellers. Transport is needed within the traveller's own country of residence and/or in an overseas destination. Many travellers also need to travel to a terminus such as an airport, railway station or ferry port before they embark on the main part of their journey.

Think back to your last holiday or day trip. How did you travel to your destination? Did you use more than one method of transport? If so, why?

Travellers require transport systems to be quick and efficient, whether they involve travel by road, rail, air or sea. Travellers today expect to be able to travel far and wide and their choice of transport depends on several factors. These include:

Price Today, with the introduction of low-cost air carriers such as easyJet, Ryanair and bmibaby, people can now reach European destinations that

Budget airlines have made air travel much more affordable

previously were too expensive to reach. For example, a return flight to Dublin from a UK airport in the early part of this century could cost anything between £200 and £300. Now the budget airlines can do the same journey for as little as £29 return.

Those travelling for leisure purposes rather than for business may choose not to travel during peak times in order to take advantage of cheaper fares offered by train companies, for example.

Think about it

On the same scheduled flight to exactly the same destination, passengers will have paid different amounts of money for their ticket depending on which class they travel in. Why do you think some passengers are willing to pay more to travel in business or first class rather than in economy class?

Destination Not all destinations are serviced by a range of transport providers and a traveller's choice may be limited by this. An example of this is tourists visiting some of the smaller Greek islands. They may fly into Athens airport but then have to transfer to a ferry to reach their holiday destination. This is because the island that is their final destination has no airport.

Time How much time a traveller has available to them can dictate their choice of transportation. A week's leisurely holiday along the canals of East Anglia may be a holiday idyll for some travellers. The chance to meander along waterways in a barge only covering thirty miles in a week is ideal for the relaxed holidaymaker, but for a business

person travelling the length and breadth of the UK, speed is of the essence. Speed in this case would, ultimately, be the key to choosing a travel and transport provider.

Reason Visiting friends or relatives, business or leisure.

The need for speed, the time available to travel and the reason to travel, all combine to influence a traveller's choice of travel and transport provider. As for price, business travellers may be prepared to pay more for their travel, if it is necessary for getting their work done efficiently and because they may not be personally responsible for the costs, as their companies will be paying. To reduce costs and to benefit from bulk-buying discounts, companies often have special arrangements with certain transport providers to provide services at specially negotiated prices.

Departure points How easy is it to get to a departure point? For example, if a small town had a bus/coach station but not a railway station, then travellers in that area may not see travelling by train as a viable option.

Skills practice

Draw an outline of a map of the UK. Mark on your map the main air and ferry ports.

Skills practice

A new airport was opened in South Yorkshire in March 2005. Formerly RAF Finningley, the new airport is named the Robin Hood Doncaster/Sheffield airport.

Try to find out about the new airport and why it was opened? Answer the following questions:

1 How can this new airport be accessed? Consider both road and rail links.

2 Why do you think a new airport was opened in this area?

3 Demand for air travel has grown in recent years. Why do you think this is?

4 Many existing airports want to extend and build additional runways. Local residents are opposed to these plans. What arguments would you use to justify extending our airports?

The development of transport systems

The development of transport systems can be attributed to technological advances. During the reign of Queen Victoria in the 1800s, travelling by steam train was seen as a major technological breakthrough in travel, however many people were nervous of a machine that could travel at speeds of up to thirty miles per hour. It wasn't until the Queen travelled by train herself that many people's fears were allayed about the dangers of such speeds!

The introduction of the steam train, the motorcar and the jet engine have all contributed to the growth of travel systems and the organisations that provide transportation for travellers.

The role of transport providers is integral to the whole tourism industry in physically moving tourists and travellers to and around their destinations.

Figure 1.6 Transport providers of the travel and tourism industry

Research could be conducted by visiting an organisation's website, writing to them or interviewing an employee of the business.

The Bal family

Raj, Rapinder and their two children, Kuldeep and Gurjit, are eagerly awaiting their forthcoming trip to Florida to visit some of the world's most famous theme parks.

Naturally the children are excited about the trip, but Rapinder is worrying about the amount of travel involved. The family will fly out of Manchester Airport and when they arrive in the USA, their hotel is approximately a seventy-five-minute drive from the airport. The family have a fly/drive package organised by their local travel agent in Wakefield.

1 **List all the methods of transport you think the family will need to use for this trip. Consider every part of their journey.**
2 **For each of the methods of transport you have listed in Task 1, write about why you consider that method the most appropriate.**
3 **For families travelling with young children, what type of services would you expect transport providers to offer?**
4 **Price may not be the most influential factor taken into account by young families when deciding on transport to a particular destination. Discuss the extent to which you agree with this statement. Explain your answer fully.**

Skills practice

National Express are a coach company which runs services all over the UK. Visit the organisation's website to research the destinations and departure points serviced by the company.

Once you have a 'feel' for the organisation, answer the following questions:

1 Who are National Express' customers?

2 Who do you consider to be National Express' main competitors?
3 With increasing congestion on our roads and more stringent environmental laws being made, how do you think National Express can move forward into the future?

CASE STUDY
'Le Chunnel'

The Channel Tunnel was opened in the early 1990s, finally linking mainland UK to continental Europe. With a terminus in Ashford, Kent, at the end of the M20 motorway and one at Waterloo railway station in London, travellers can travel directly to European cities in the comfort of their own cars or a high-speed train (Eurostar).

The concept of a tunnel under the English Channel had been dreamt of for many years. Attempts to link England and France had been made since Napoleonic times. Resistance to the tunnel being built came from local residents in Kent and ferry operators feared they would lose customers and, ultimately, profit.

Though it is a major feat of modern engineering, the Channel Tunnel has been controversial and rarely out of the media spotlight. It is used by the white van brigade as the main route for transporting into this country the cheaper alcohol and cigarettes they buy in France. Industrial action and fires have disrupted services to passengers and the tunnel has become a favourite route of illegal immigrants into the UK.

1 Why do you think the Channel Tunnel is a popular route with many travellers?

2 As a cross-channel ferry operator, how would you tackle competition from the Channel Tunnel?

3 Safety has obviously been an issue in the Channel Tunnel, given that vehicles have caught fire whilst in the tunnel. On the list of travellers' requirements, safety is paramount. Imagine you are working as a marketing manager for the Channel Tunnel, devise a marketing campaign designed to promote the tunnel as a safe means of transport.

4 Eurostar is the name of the high-speed train which takes travellers from London to continental Europe. Use your research skills to find out where in Europe the Eurostar travels to.

5 The Channel Tunnel employs approximately 5000 people. What type of job opportunities do you think are offered by the Channel Tunnel?

Accommodation providers

Where to stay and how much to pay for accommodation are factors in choosing where to holiday and visit for many tourists. After transportation, this is possibly the second-most crucial part of the industry and many people are employed in a variety of different job roles. From top quality hotels offering every luxury imaginable to a youth hostel offering a bed in a shared dormitory, the traveller has many options of where to stay.

Below is a diagram showing examples of different types of accommodation. This is not meant to be exhaustive.

Think about it

For each of the types of accommodation listed, try and write a definition.

Location is usually important to travellers when choosing accommodation. Finding accommodation in exactly the right place can be tricky and often very pricey. Certain types of accommodation are only available in certain locations. For example, gîtes are only found in rural areas of France. Location also affects the type of accommodation on offer. For example, in a city location there is likely to be a wide range of hotels, from five-star luxury to small

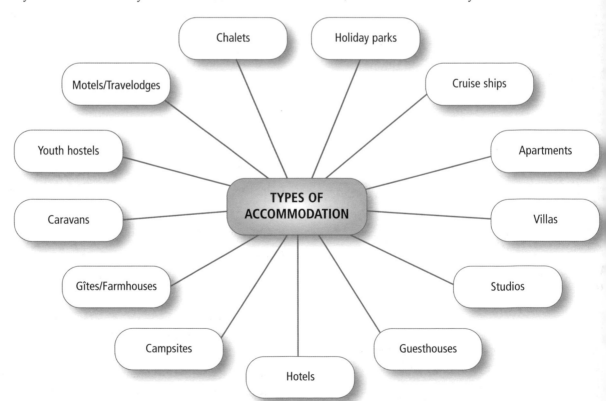

Figure 1.7 Types of accommodation in the travel and tourism industry

independently owned hotels. In cities you are also more likely to find hotels that belong to a chain. Lots of hotel chains today are not only national but also international and can be found in a number of destinations in a number of countries. Examples of these include Holiday Inn, Ibis, Marriott, Sheraton and Hilton.

Smaller towns and rural areas are more likely to offer guesthouses and bed and breakfast accommodation facilities. Some rural areas offer country house hotel accommodation, combining the luxury of top city hotels with the genteel rural life and settings. Seaside resorts offer a mixture of accommodation: hotels, guesthouses, flats and caravan sites. Hotels can be categorised according to their location:

* City centre hotels

* Beach hotels

* Resort hotels

* Country house hotels.

A *country house hotel combines luxury with a rural setting*

Skills practice

Tourists have different needs and different budgets. For each of the types of hotel write a profile in terms of age, socio-economic grouping, activities, likes and dislikes.

CASE STUDY

The Crouches – taking a baby on a holiday

Jonathan and Donna have recently had their first baby, Rowan. To take full advantage of Donna's maternity leave, the family are planning to go on a relaxing holiday for a week in the Spanish holiday resort of Fuengirola. Jonathan wants to stay in a hotel so that neither he nor Donna have to cook. When the family travel, Rowan will be six months old.

1   As a family with a young child, the Crouches will have many specific requirements. Create a list of as many requirements you can think of that will meet the needs of the Crouch family.

2   The Crouches want to stay in a hotel. What type of facilities do you think the hotel will need to have to meet the requirements of the family?

3   Log on to the website of one of the major travel agents and find a hotel that is suitable for the family to stay in. Remember their requirements and fully price the cost of the holiday.

Accommodation can be divided into two categories:

* *Serviced accommodation* – where meals are provided, for example hotels and guesthouses

* *Self-catering accommodation* – such as farmhouses, chalets and some hotels.

In serviced accommodation, tourists may have a choice of eating arrangements to choose from. The options available include:

* Full board – also known as the 'American Plan', three meals a day are provided for tourists

* All-inclusive – the cost of food and snacks and a selection of drinks is included in the price of the holiday

* Half-board – known as the 'modified American plan', breakfast and one other meal is offered to guests

* Bed and breakfast – known as the 'Continental plan', tourists pay for their room and their breakfast. The cost of other meals is extra.

Price can also be a contributing factor in a traveller's choice of accommodation. The price of accommodation is determined by the facilities on offer. The more and better the facilities are, the more it costs to stay. Accommodation is usually graded to help tourists in making their decision. There are a number of organisations that accredit hotels, for example the RAC and the AA both classify a large number of hotels, bed and breakfasts and guesthouses, and travellers use these as a guide to the quality and facilities on offer. The English Tourism Council also visits a wide range of tourist accommodation and annually assesses accommodation, so tourists can be confident that where they are staying has been thoroughly checked out. All the assessing bodies use these general guidelines when grading accommodation in terms of quality:

* A star rating of between one and five stars is awarded to hotels and self-catering accommodation. Stars are awarded for quality in terms of décor and furnishings and for facilities such as lifts, swimming pools, and entertainment systems in bedrooms. The greater number of stars awarded, the better the facilities and services offered.

* Holiday, touring and camping parks inspected by the English Tourism Council are also given ratings of between one and five stars. The AA, however, awards pennants (flags) for the same types of accommodation. With both schemes, the number awarded is based on the quality of service, cleanliness, environment and facilities provided.

* Other accommodation, such as guesthouses, bed and breakfasts, inns and farmhouses, are awarded between one and five diamonds. Again, the more diamonds that are awarded, the better quality of the services and facilities provided.

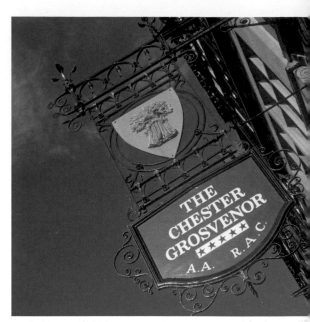

The use of stars is one way tourist accommodation is graded

Skills practice

You work for the RAC as a hotel inspector. You travel the length and breadth of the country, visiting hotels and awarding them with stars. The better the accommodation, the more stars awarded.

You are looking to be promoted and have been asked to rewrite the evaluation form used by inspectors when assessing hotels. This you feel is your opportunity to really impress your bosses.

It is your task therefore to write a new evaluation form considering all the different aspects you may be looking for when awarding ratings.

Skills practice

Following on from your task to write a new evaluation form for hotel inspectors, visit a local hotel and use your form to assess the facilities on offer.

Remember to ask permission from the manager.

Skills practice

City Hotels, an international chain of hotels, has asked you, a renowned hotel designer, to decide on the facilities to be installed in its newest hotel development. The new hotel will be located in Liverpool and is aimed at business people during the week and families at the weekend.

Tour operators

Every year when it comes to deciding where to go on holiday, we find ourselves flicking through a number of brochures, looking for the perfect holiday destination.

Weighing up the relative merits and demerits of each resort and type of accommodation, where we can fly from and at what time of day the flights are, we give little thought as to how the whole package is organised. Tour operators are responsible for combining the key elements of a holiday, namely transport and accommodation, into the package holiday, which we spend so much time choosing.

There are two main types of tour operators:

* *Wholesale operators* – these put together and organise package holidays that are then only sold through retail travel agents.

* *Direct sell operators* – these do not use travel agents as facilitators in selling their packages, but sell their package holidays direct to the general public.

Tour operators generally specialise in domestic, outbound or inbound travel. Domestic tour operators arrange packages to destinations within the UK; outbound tour operators arrange packages to overseas destinations; and inbound tour operators arrange packages for overseas visitors visiting the UK. Some tour operators provide both domestic and outbound package holidays, for example Wallace Arnold.

The role of tour operators is to act as the intermediaries or 'wholesalers' in the retail distribution chain. They provide, for example, the link between the hotels, airlines and the travel agents on the high street, where we book our holidays.

Tour operators have traditionally had considerable control over the types of destinations visited by travellers as they are responsible for planning and marketing holidays to selected destinations. The role of tour operators is varied and complex and comprises the following activities:

* Organising travel and accommodation

* Setting prices for holidays based on budgeted costs of a package

* Producing marketing materials, especially brochures advertising the holidays arranged

* Distributing brochures to travel agents.

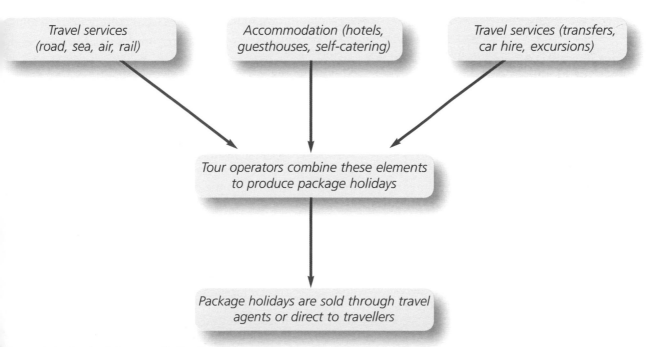

Figure 1.8 The holiday retail distribution chain

The process of organising a package holiday has to be done well in advance of any customer's commitment to purchase. Customers expect all the planning and organisation to have been done so that they are buying a package that is complete and ready to be used and enjoyed. Working in conjunction with travel agents, tour operators aim to provide 'hassle-free' holidaying for the traveller. Brochures promoting the holidays are printed anything from six months to a year in advance of when holidays will actually be taken, which also meets the needs of customers who like to book their preferred choice well in advance.

The first step in putting together a package holiday is the selection of resorts and destinations by tour operators. Larger tour operators have marketing departments which research current market trends to find out what customers want, how much they are willing to spend, how far they are willing to travel and how many want to visit new destinations. In recent years tour operators have extended their offerings beyond the much-loved Spanish resorts and islands, to destinations such as the Greek islands, Florida and Mexico.

Think about it

Why do you think resorts such as Florida and Cancun in Mexico have become more popular with tourists from the UK?

Tour operators generally select organisations on the basis of five essential criteria:

1 Accessibility
2 Attractions
3 Quality of local facilities and services
4 Availability of excursions
5 Political stability of the area.

Skills practice

Select one of the following destinations: Cancun in Mexico, Skanes in Tunisia or Eilat in Egypt. For the resort you have chosen, use the five essential criteria used by tour operators to make a judgement on how suitable these resorts are to be offered to customers.

Accommodation selected by tour operators has to be checked well in advance for its suitability for the tour operators' customers. Tour operators generally guarantee hotel owners that they will take a number of rooms in advance. These rooms in selected accommodation are then featured in brochures.

Skills practice

Imagine you work for one of the major tour operators selecting hotels and self-catering accommodation in a number of popular tourist destinations. You have been asked to create a new checklist to be used in assessing the suitability of accommodation. It is your task to create this checklist, taking into consideration factors such as facilities, star rating, location and proximity to beaches.

Brochures are not only marketing materials that aim to persuade travellers to choose the package holidays of one particular tour operator, they also need to be informative. Travellers rely on tour operators to provide them with all the information they need to know about a particular destination. This can range from entry requirements (e.g. visas), health regulations (vaccinations needed), time zones, currency used, language spoken, local festivals and bank holidays, and any other information relating to local culture and customs.

Skills practice

Mauritius is an island in the Indian Ocean. You work for a major tour operator who is extending the number of destinations they offer and Mauritius is to be included as one of the new destinations for next year. Your task is to research the island and create the text to be included in the brochure to inform travellers about the destination. You need to research:

• Entry requirements
• Health regulations
• Time zones
• Currency used
• Language spoken
• Local festivals
• Local culture and customs.

Costing package holidays can be very difficult for tour operators. The most difficult to cost is air travel. Tour operators charter flights up to eighteen months in advance and these need to be 80 per cent occupied if the tour operator is to cover the costs. Flight costs are especially hard to calculate as the cost of aviation fuel can vary enormously depending on external factors which tour operators have no control over, such as the supply of aviation fuel, political situations, taxation and the general state of the economy.

Value for money and quality are features which most customers are looking for when choosing holidays. Tour operators must convince customers that their products and services are value for money. When tour operators calculate the cost of holidays, they consider the following.

* The type of accommodation – is it serviced or self-catering?

* The number in the party – different rates are charged for children and discounts can be given for larger groups.

* The type of transport used – to get to some destinations and resorts, a variety of modes of transport may be needed.

* The point of departure – where the traveller leaves from at the start of their journey.

* The time of year – during the summer when the weather is usually better in most resorts and during peak times such as school holidays, tour operators charge more as there is greater demand for their products and services.

Once tour operators have completed the organisation and planning of package holidays they have to sell them to travel agents who will in turn sell them to the general public. Tour operators visit travel agents to update them on the range of holidays offered. Travel agents will then sell the tour operators' holidays and receive a commission, usually a percentage of sales, in return. Occasionally, larger operators will send travel agent staff to particular resorts to promote holidays offered by that tour operator.

Apart from the services offered to travellers before they depart for their holiday destination, many tour operators offer services when they arrive. The most common service is that of resort representatives. Their role is to welcome guests, organise excursions and deal with any emergencies guests may have. Representatives

CASE STUDY

July and August – the most expensive months of the year

'Have you seen the difference in prices?'

Andy was not impressed that the same holiday he had selected from the new brochure of 'Go Far' was £450 more expensive in July than in May. Granted that July is always warmer than May, but why the difference in price for one week in the same three-star hotel in Torremolinos, Spain?

Andy and Jill and their three children were planning their annual holiday, but were utterly dismayed by the cost in the school summer holidays. The cost of the holiday in July was too high for the family's limited budget and Andy made the following decision.

'We're going in May. The greedy tour operators are not ripping me off. The kids can miss a week of school!'

1 Why do you think tour operators charge more for holidays during school holidays?

2 Do you think it is ethical for tour operators to charge more for holidays when they know demand will be greater for their products and services?

3 Many families feel they have no alternative but to take children out of school during term time. Other people believe that this is wrong. How could overseas travel contribute to a child's education?

also monitor the quality of the tour operator's services and customers' opinions whilst on holiday.

Large tour operators tend to organise package holidays to the most popular resorts, whilst smaller tour operators tend to specialise in offering packages that fill a niche in the market that meet specific needs. For example, there are tour operators who specialise in packages for travellers who want to participate in a range of extreme sports. There are also operators specialising in packages to specific destinations such as Australia and New Zealand.

Skills practice

You can use a spreadsheet package for this activity to practise your ICT skills.

1 Create a list of twenty tour operators.

2 For each of the tour operators, state whether they offer domestic, outbound or inbound package holidays. Remember some may offer a combination of more than one type of package holiday.

3 Add to your list whether the tour operator is a wholesale tour operator or a direct seller.

Despite the availability of tour operators, there are travellers who prefer to arrange their own holidays. This is getting easier as people become more confident about travelling and as they get accustomed to booking holidays through the Internet.

Think about it

What do you think are the advantages of travelling independently?

Travel agents

The travel agent's role is that of 'retailer'. Travel agents sell holidays on behalf of tour operators as well as selling other products and services supplied by principals, such as airline tickets and hotel bookings. They also sell and provide other products and services, including travel insurance, currency exchange, traveller's cheques, guided tours and tickets for entertainments. As travel agents are selling holidays to the general public they tend to be located in areas where there is high customer traffic, such as high streets and major centres in towns and cities.

Skills practice

Visit your local high street or shopping centre to conduct a survey about the number of travel agents located there and the products and services they offer.

The main aims of travel agents are:

✱ to sell holidays and associated products such as insurance, car hire and currency exchange

✱ to advise clients

✱ to provide information.

Travel agents sell their products and services in much the same way as most other retailers on the high street. However, as they are selling the products of other companies (such as airlines, hotels, rail companies, tour operators) they are only paid a commission by those companies on the money they receive from the customers.

Travel agents either specialise in a particular market or sell a wide range of products and services to a wide range of people. The travel agents who specialise in selling holidays to Australia, for example, are usually independents, not part of a national chain. Even a travel agent

A travel agent sells holidays and associated products, advises clients and provides information

who has up to six shops/offices can be classed as independent. Independents are generally located in smaller premises in suburban or village locations and often in less prominent positions, such as above another retail outlet.

Travel agents that are part of a larger nationwide chain are known as multiples. Examples include Thomas Cook and Lunn Poly. These offer a wide range of products and services to a wide range of destinations and resorts. They are also retail travel agents, not just business travel agents who arrange business trips. Business travel agents operate in much the same way as retail travel agents, in booking flights and accommodation for their clients. Large organisations such as Boots Plc and Marks & Spencer have their own business travel agents to arrange travel and accommodation for their staff. Profits are often higher for business travel agents but many trips are arranged at short notice.

Think about it

What are the key differences between independent and multiple travel agents?

Skills practice

Write definitions for the following:
- Retail travel agent
- Business travel agent
- Independent travel agent
- Multiple travel agent.

Skills practice

Refer back to the second section of this unit, 'The development of travel and tourism'. Technological advances, such as central reservation systems, have impacted on the work of travel agents. How do you think these systems have helped travel agents and what are the advantages and disadvantages of using the systems?

To protect tourists from the unscrupulous, all travel agents are required to hold a licence from the International Air Transport Association (IATA) to sell airline tickets. Travel agents may also register with the Association of British Travel Agents (ABTA) to improve their reputation and to provide customers with a guarantee that they will not lose money if the travel agency goes out of business.

Skills practice

ABTA is an association to help protect travellers from losing money if a travel agency stops trading or from being stranded overseas if one of the travel principals goes out of business.

Research the role ABTA plays in the travel and tourism industry by finding out in detail what the association stands for and how it operates.

Travel agents – the future

For many years, travel agents were where most travellers went to book a holiday. The boom years for travel agents were the 1960s–1980s when all sorts of people started to travel overseas on package tours to popular destinations such as Spain, Balearic Islands and the Canary Islands. The travel agent was seen as a 'one-stop shop', where the traveller could book their holiday, buy insurance, change their currency and book a car parking space at the airport. The last twenty years has seen more people booking their holidays and arranging their own travel arrangements independently. One of the major reasons for travellers becoming more independent in planning their travel, itineraries and accommodation, is undoubtedly the growth of the Internet and personal computer ownership.

Threats to traditional travel agents

The travel agency sector of the travel and tourism industry is highly competitive. However, the major threat to travel agents today is technology, as it enables travellers to become more independent and dispense with the services of the travel agent.

Think about it

Technology is a threat to travel agents. What other threats do you think travel agents face today?

Imagine you are the managing director of a small chain of four travel agents in your local area. You need to put together a one-page summary of how you are going to react to threats facing travel agents. Your summary needs to include:

- A list of what you consider to be threats to your business

- What products and services you will offer to make you stand out from the competition

- How you will price the products and services you sell

- How you will promote your business to ensure customers will keep using your services.

CASE STUDY

Anne – 13 years in the business

Anne has worked in the travel agency business for more than thirteen years. She has always worked for the larger nationwide chains of travel agents and has recently been interviewed to give a real insight into the life of a travel agent, the changes that have impacted on the industry and what the future holds for traditional high street travel agents.

Hayley: Anne, you've worked in a travel agency for a long time now, what do you think have been the major changes since you started work in the industry?

Anne: It's now thirteen years I've been working as a travel agent. I started work for Lunn Poly as soon as I left school at sixteen. Things are so different now to when I first started working. The main difference is the customers. People are so demanding these days and customers know what they are talking about. People have travelled more and are more experienced. They know what type of holiday they want and how much everything costs. Of course, customer knowledge is no bad thing, but people are always quoting prices from other travel agents, and especially from the Internet travel companies.

Hayley: So the Internet has had a real impact on your business then?

Anne: The Internet has had a massive impact on the amount of business we do. It's made a really big difference. Price is the main way that the Internet travel companies have affected our business. They can offer holidays cheaper than we can as they don't have the same costs and overheads to cover. We have to pay for staff, shop rental, electricity, etc.

Hayley: If travel agents can't compete on price, how can they compete with such fierce rivals?

Anne: We can compete on price to a certain extent. Where I work now, we have a price watch promise and we can match quotes of other high street travel agents. As for the Internet travel companies, we can offer the face-to-face contact that they can't. There's also still a whole generation, particularly older people, who don't know how to use computers or don't have one at home, and it's these people who still use our services. It'll probably be different though in the next ten to twenty years as technology will become even cheaper and everybody will have access to the Internet.

Hayley: The future for high street travel agents is okay then?

Anne: I wouldn't go that far! In the future, we'll see less and less of what we see now on the high street. I think most travel agents will either become huge holiday supermarkets or telephone call centres with no shops. Competition is fierce now and I think it'll get worse as customers become more sophisticated and price sensitive.

Hayley: Do people demand different products and services today than they did thirteen years ago?

Anne: Yeah, people are much more adventurous today. They want to go further afield and the Caribbean has become really popular. People also like to go to places like that to get married. They are guaranteed good weather and don't have to invite members of the family they never see to the wedding!

Hayley: Apart from the increase in long-haul destinations, what other changes have you noticed?

Anne: A real noticeable change has been the increase in cruising. When I first started work, cruises were for the over-sixties but now they are aimed at the family market. People like the idea of everything being under one roof and visiting different places in one holiday. Modern ships are huge and the entertainment is non-stop. It's a bit like an upmarket floating Butlins holiday resort with sports and activities organised by a team of staff.

Hayley: Has the technology used in shops changed much?

Anne: No, not really. We've had new computers and I suppose communication lines don't go down and fail as much as they used to, but the reservation systems we use are more or less the same as they were when I started working. Travel agents invested loads of money years ago into reservation systems and the like, but little has been spent in recent times. Costs are always being cut and I don't think updating systems is a priority at the moment. It's a real pain when systems do fail though. It's really embarrassing when you have a client with you and you have to try and get through on the telephone. It also takes ages as if a system crashes, it usually crashes nationally and every travel agent is trying to book holidays over the telephone. Sometimes you can even lose customers as they are annoyed that the system has crashed. Our shop doesn't even have its own email link. It's a real pain.

Hayley: What events outside of your control have had an impact on business?

Anne: Without a doubt the latest conflict in Iraq and the Gulf has had a real impact on business. Coupled with 9/11, these two events have made people more apprehensive to travel. Also people don't want to travel to destinations in the Middle East, such as Dubai, as they are scared of terrorist attacks. People's attitudes have changed. They now think much more about the political situation of the destinations they are travelling to, which I suppose is sensible. People generally think much more about their own personal safety and that of their family.

Hayley: Do you still enjoy working as a travel agent?

Anne: On the whole I love the job. As I said earlier, customers are so demanding but I'm sure anybody who works with the general public feels that way. Some months we are set really hard sales targets to achieve and that can really put the pressure on. The money could be better, the hours could be shorter but I'm sure that's the same with every job!

1 **What does Anne identify as major changes in the travel and tourism industry?**
2 **According to Anne, what has been the impact of Internet travel companies on traditional high street travel agents?**
3 **What does Anne believe the future will hold for travel agents?**
4 **What other external influences or events, apart from the conflict in Iraq and 9/11, do you think have had an impact on the travel and tourism industry?**
5 **Anne has worked in a travel agency for thirteen years. What skills and qualities do you think Anne needs to be able to do her job well?**

Think about it

Currency exchange has always been a service offered by travel agents to their customers. With the introduction of the Euro as the currency of many continental European countries, there has been less demand for many different types of currency. Travel agents have always charged commission to change currency. With the introduction of the Euro, do you think travel agents have had less call for their currency exchange services?

Visitor attractions

Visitor attractions provide recreation, leisure and entertainment facilities for visitors to particular destinations. The attractions vary in nature and may be provided and managed by public, private or voluntary organisations. They can be categorised into natural attractions such as country parks, purpose-built attractions such as theme parks, historic and cultural attractions such as Stonehenge, and events such as major sporting competitions like the football World Cup.

Visitor attractions can be a real 'pull' to a certain area, with visitors making special trips to the area to see a particular attraction. For example, many people visit Wiltshire to see Stonehenge, the ancient stone circles.

Stonehenge is a major historic attraction for tourists

CASE STUDY

London and the Olympic Games

London, along with other major cities in the world, is competing to hold the 2012 summer Olympic Games. Plans have been submitted to the International Olympic Committee as to how London will be redeveloped to cater for all the sporting events in the Games and how the city will cope with the number of visitors that will be drawn by the Games. Not only would new stadia have to be built but also London's transport system would need to be overhauled to be able to swiftly transport visitors around the capital.

1 **What would be the economic costs of London holding the 2012 Olympic Games?**
2 **What would be the economic benefits of London holding the 2012 Olympic Games?**
3 **How would London holding the 2012 Olympic Games be of benefit to the travel and tourism industry of the whole of the UK?**

CASE STUDY

Alton Towers

Alton Towers is the country's premier theme park, situated in Staffordshire. Originally the site of a stately home and extensive gardens, the theme park has been developed to attract thousands of visitors a year. A hotel has been built to provide accommodation and evening shows and concerts are held in the grounds of the park. Each year a new ride or attraction is added to the theme park.

1 **Why do you think the Tussauds Group, which owns Alton Towers, added a hotel to the facilities of the theme park?**
2 **Evening concerts and shows are being put on at Alton Towers. Why do you think this is so?**
3 **Alton Towers is well promoted through a series of TV advertisements. What is the purpose of spending money on such expensive campaigns?**

Support services

The role of support services depends upon the nature of the service. Support services could, for instance, include ancillary services offered as optional extras to package holidays, for example excursions and day trips. These enhance the holiday experience for the holidaymaker while offering alternative sources of income for the organisation. Representatives who work for tour operators in destination resorts offer many of these support services, and, as well as providing information and guidance to tourists in the resort, they sell excursions. Many of the representatives earn commission for the number of excursions they sell. This commission acts as an incentive for the representatives to boost their usual wage, as well as boosting revenues for tour operators.

Support services are not only provided by commercial organisations, they are also provided by public sector organisations. Tourism is seen as big business and it supports many jobs in the UK. The government has a vested interest in supporting tourism and provides support through a number of publicly funded organisations.

Think about it

What type of information do you think the English Tourism Council could provide to organisations in the travel and tourism industry to help them plan for the future?

National and regional tourist boards and information centres are funded by national and local government. These support services to the travel and tourism industry market and monitor the quality and development of the particular tourism area they serve.

Support services can be both revenue spinners and information providers for commercial

A welcome meeting for holidaymakers

organisations. Another support service is that of guiding services. The aim of guiding services is to make any guided tour as interesting and informative as possible. Guided city tours, such as open-top bus tours of London, are known throughout the world and are an attraction to tourists, enhancing their experience of a city. Many guided tours provided in stately homes and places of historic interest are led by volunteers who have a wealth of knowledge and a passion for these attractions.

The relationships between sectors and their interdependency

Being interdependent means relying on others. We all rely on others for help and support in our lives and at work; it is almost impossible to do a job without somebody else having already done another task. This idea of relying on others filters through to the travel and tourism industry, and the different sectors of the industry, described in the third section, also rely upon each other for customers and work. There are many areas of overlap in the industry and many organisations depend directly upon the activities and success of others.

The success of tour operators and the number of holidays they sell depends very much on how well travel agents are promoting the products and services of the tour operator and how successful they are at persuading customers to purchase particular holidays. If the travel agent is not selling holidays, then neither is the tour operator, thus illustrating the interdependency of these two sectors. Another example is visitor attractions experiencing a downturn in the number of visitors due to problems with transport systems and accessibility.

As a tour operator you may be concerned about the way in which travel agents sell your products and services, especially if a travel agent is also selling the products and services of other tour operators. The travel agent may in turn be concerned about the quality of service offered by an airline that it sells tickets for. If the quality of service from the airline is poor, then the reputation of the travel agent could be damaged as it is seen as recommending inferior services to its customers. Travel agents may also be put in a compromising position if they send customers to a hotel that is not of a very high standard.

Customers trust the different sectors of the travel and tourism industry to provide them with value-for-money products and services. However, because the different principals involved in providing a holiday – tour operator, travel agent, hotelier – can be individual, unrelated companies, each of the organisations involved could have conflicting aims and objectives for what they want to achieve. To gain more control over the whole chain of the holiday experience, several organisations have become vertically integrated.

Vertical integration occurs when a single company extends its activities into another stage of the distribution process. A company may wish to gain a controlling interest in a tour operation, a travel agency and an airline. This enables the company to sell its own products without paying commission and gives it priority in purchasing airline seats. It also allows significant economies of scale, lowering costs because of the increased purchasing power of a larger organisation. Examples of vertical integration include

Thomas Cook, the travel agent owning the Iberostar hotel chain with hotels in the 'summer sun' resorts and the Thomas Cook airline, and the Thomson tour operator owning Britannia airlines.

Think about it

What do you foresee as some of the problems of vertical integration?

Skills practice

As a director of a tour operator, you are concerned about the future of your organisation and see vertical integration as a way of gaining control over the sale of your holidays in uncertain times for the travel and tourism industry. Your task is to prepare a presentation to persuade the other directors that vertical integration is the best option to take the business forward.

In your presentation you need to include the following:

- An explanation of what vertical integration is
- Examples of how your tour operator could vertically integrate with other sectors
- The advantages of vertical integration
- The disadvantages of vertical integration (to show that you appreciate the limitations of vertical integration as well as the benefits)
- Your plans – how you aim to vertically integrate.

Skills practice

There have been concerns that vertical integration of organisations in different sectors of the travel and tourism industry leaves the customer with less choice. Some cases of organisations integrating have been taken to the Competition Commission.

1 What is the role of the Competition Commission?

2 Why do you think there is a need for such a body as the Competition Commission?

3 Can you think of an example of integration in the travel and tourism industry that may be stopped from going ahead in the interests of maintaining competitiveness in the market?

Many organisations have sought vertical integration, giving them greater control of all aspects of their business. One of the major reasons behind seeking vertical integration is to provide a wider range of products and services and to offer a more extensive portfolio of products. Careful planning and marketing of all products and services is needed to ensure that all processes in the distribution channel are well managed and that quality, value for money and service is maintained.

Think about it

As well as vertical integration, organisations in the travel and tourism industry can integrate horizontally. What do you think this means?

UNIT ASSESSMENT

The aim of this section is to help prepare you for your external examination by having you answer a variety of questions on the material covered for this unit. You will be required to demonstrate your knowledge, apply this knowledge to vocational contexts, analyse information and perform evaluations based on these skills.

Defining travel and tourism

1 Name the three main types of tourism. (3 marks)

2 What is the difference between the three main types of tourism? (6 marks)

3   What are the three main reasons why people travel? (3 marks)

4   The following table includes data collected about overseas visitors to the UK and the purpose of their visit.

COUNTRY	LEISURE VISITS (000s)	BUSINESS VISITS (000s)	VISITING FRIENDS AND RELATIVES (000s)
Australia	355	75	240
Canada	246	83	266
France	1085	1112	695
Germany	1130	853	552
India	75	51	38
Italy	396	331	171
Japan	292	111	32
Spain	249	263	201
USA	1876	851	803

Adapted from *Number of visits, nights and spending by overseas visitors to the UK 1999*, Office for National Statistics

a   What does the above data set show? (1 mark)

b   This data set contains data collected on the three main purposes of travel. List two other reasons why people may travel. (2 marks)

c   From the data provided, which is the main reason for why people travel to the UK? (1 mark)

d   In what units have the number of visits to the UK been measured? (2 marks)

e   What factors do you think have an impact on the number of travellers from other countries to the UK? (6 marks)

f   The UK is thought by people in many countries to be a very expensive country to visit. If the pound is strong against other currencies, what will be the likely effect on the number of tourists visiting the UK? Explain your answer fully. (8 marks)

g   Working for the British Tourism Authority, you are devising a new marketing campaign to attract overseas visitors to the UK. Why do you think public money is invested in promoting the UK as a tourist destination? (6 marks)

5 Many tourists from the UK choose to holiday overseas. The data below shows the countries visited by UK tourists in 1999.

COUNTRY	PERCENTAGE
Spain	27
France	20
USA	7
Greece	6
Eire	6
Italy	4
Portugal	4
Cyprus	2
Netherlands	2
Turkey	2
Belgium	2
Caribbean	2
Germany	2
North Africa	1
Other countries	1

Adapted from *International Passenger Survey*,
Office for National Statistics 1999

a Which country was most visited by UK tourists in 1999? (1 mark)

b In the category of other countries, give two examples of destinations that this may include. (2 marks)

c European destinations appear to be very popular with UK tourists. What factors do you think contribute to this popularity? (6 marks)

d Using an example of a resort you have studied, describe the attractions in that resort that may attract tourists from the UK. (8 marks)

e Domestic tourism has become more popular in the early twenty-first century, with more people choosing to holiday at home. What events do you think have led to this recent trend? (8 marks)

6 What is the difference between organisations in the private, public and voluntary sectors of the travel and tourism industry? (4 marks)

7 Using an example of an external pressure on the travel and tourism industry, evaluate the impact that pressure has had on tourism. (8 marks)

8 Host communities both gain and lose from the development of tourism in their areas. To what extent do you agree with this statement? (12 marks)

The development of the travel and tourism industry

1   What influence do you think Thomas Cook had on the travel and tourism industry in the UK? (8 marks)

2   There is no longer a need for traditional high street travel agents due to the emergence of online travel companies. Evaluate the extent to which you believe this statement to be correct. (12 marks)

3   Tourism is an activity which the majority of the population can today access. What historical developments have led to tourism for the masses rather than just for the wealthy elite? (8 marks)

4   Travellers today are becoming much more sophisticated, confident and independent. How do you think travellers have reached this point? (8 marks)

5   The travel and tourism industry is dynamic and forever evolving. What do you think will be future developments in the industry? Fully explain your answer. (8 marks)

Different sectors of the travel and tourism industry

1   Name the six different sectors of the travel and tourism industry. (6 marks)

2   What factors are taken into consideration by a tourist when choosing transportation? (4 marks)

3   What is the purpose of grading schemes for accommodation in the travel and tourism industry? (4 marks)

4   With the increase of online travel companies, there will be an increase in the number of direct sell tour operators. To what extent do you believe this statement to be true? (12 marks)

Relationships between sectors and their interdependency

1   Sectors in the travel and tourism industry are said to be interdependent. What does this mean? (4 marks)

2   Explain how organisations in the travel and tourism industry depend directly upon the activities and success of others. (6 marks)

3   What is vertical integration? (3 marks)

4   Using an example of a company you have studied, describe the benefits and drawbacks of vertically integrated companies in the travel and tourism industry. (12 marks)

Total marks: 180

Travel and tourism – a people industry

Introduction

This unit introduces you to customer service as provided by travel and tourism organisations. It shows you why it is important for these organisations to provide excellent customer service in an industry where organisations offer similar products and services to each other. It is usually the quality of customer service that is the deciding factor as to which organisation customers use. Owners and managers therefore need to view customer service as necessary to the survival, development and success of the organisation.

The unit helps you understand how important training and induction are in preparing staff to provide customer service. You also learn how important a good level of product knowledge is in providing high levels of customer service. Finally, you will learn that customers have different needs and that the customer service skills you develop can be applied to a variety of situations in which customers' needs have to be met.

> ### How you will be assessed

The unit is assessed by portfolio evidence based on an investigation into aspects of customer service in a chosen travel and tourism organisation.

Your portfolio should include:

* A review of induction procedures and training provided by your chosen organisation
* A record of customer service role plays, demonstrating how you would meet the needs of different types of customer of your chosen travel and tourism organisation
* An investigation into the product knowledge required by employees of the organisation
* An evaluation of the range of skills required to deliver customer service.

After studying this unit you need to have learned:

* The principles of customer service
* The needs of internal and external customers
* The significance of induction and training
* The significance of product knowledge
* The importance of customer service skills
* Dealing with different types of customer
* The technical skills that contribute to operating effectively in travel and tourism organisations.

Through studying this unit you will acquire valuable skills and understanding which you can use in studying other units in the AS Double Award: Unit 4 Working in Travel and Tourism and Unit 5 Travel and Tourism. For the A2 qualification understanding and the practice of customer service skills will be necessary for Unit 8 Marketing in Travel and Tourism and Unit 9 Travel and Tourism – People and Quality, which are both compulsory units. This unit therefore provides essential skills and understanding to achieve success in the AS and A2 qualifications.

What is customer service?

A *customer* is an individual with specific needs when buying products and services and expects a very high level of service in meeting those needs. *Customer service* involves providing products and services that meet the needs of the customer and satisfy their demands. This particularly applies to travel and tourism – a people industry – where the success of any business depends on providing customers with a high level of customer service.

Customer service is crucial to the success of a travel and trourism business

CASE STUDY

Customer service at the travel agents

There are three travel agents in town and Sophie and Rick decide to visit all three to find the best deal for a two-week holiday in Bulgaria.

The first travel agent had a dazzling window display showing all the late deals and special offers. It looked very inviting. Everyone else must have thought the same as there must have been ten other people waiting to see the one travel consultant on duty.

Sophie and Rick were greeted with 'Take a seat. Both my colleagues are at lunch but they will be back in forty-five minutes. Feel free to look at the brochures.'

Rick and Sophie moved on to the next travel agent.

This one was just off the high street. It too had an enticing window display showing promises of free insurance and commission-free currency exchange. There was only one member of staff on duty and she was working on a computer. Sophie and Rick sat down and waited for the travel consultant to finish her work on the computer. This lasted five minutes and they still hadn't been greeted with an 'Hello' or 'Be with you in one minute.'

The consultant was about to turn her attention to them when the phone rang. Again no apology to her two clients. A five-minute conversation with head office followed.

Finally, after putting some more chewing gum in her mouth, she was ready to focus on Sophie and Rick, who were already on their way out.

Third time lucky was what Sophie and Rick thought. The third travel agency was again busy but at least there were three consultants dealing with their clients. One of them greeted Sophie and Rick with a smile and asked them to take a seat, saying they would be attended to as soon as possible.

Rick helped himself to a free cup of coffee and they both watched a promotional video about the products and services the travel agency offered.

After about three minutes a very welcoming travel consultant apologised for the wait and invited them to her desk. She asked what type of holiday Sophie and Rick were looking for, the price range they were aiming at, the type of accommodation they preferred and the airport they wanted to fly from. Throughout the conversation the travel consultant was making eye contact, listening closely and thinking about what would match Sophie and Rick's needs. And all this time, she never once looked at her computer!

1 **How could the customer service be improved in the first two travel agents?**
2 **Why is it important to treat customers appropriately?**

Skills practice

When customers visit a travel and tourism organisation for the first time they tend to react to two things: the staff and the physical surroundings. The first reaction is to the tangible, i.e. what they perceive through their senses; the second is to the non-tangible, i.e. the emotional effect. Examples of the tangible are staff uniforms and the directional signs; examples of the non-tangible are the friendliness of staff and the atmosphere.

On your own, list some of the features that might create a pleasant visit for
- a family group visiting a theme park
- a guest in a hotel
- a passenger on an aeroplane.

Think about it

One way of knowing if customers are satisfied with the service they received in a restaurant is the amount of tips in the 'tips' jar. An empty jar is not encouraging!

Think about other ways which show that customers have been happy with the service they received.

In recent times the UK economy has increasingly moved away from the primary and secondary sectors towards the service sector. Travel and tourism plays a major part in the service sector in that it employs thousands of people and is totally geared towards providing the services that its customers need and want.

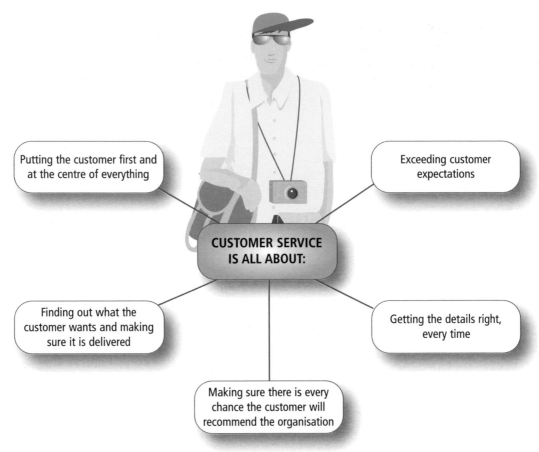

Figure 2.1 This is what customer service is all about

Organisations that fail to appreciate that customers must come first, will find themselves inundated with complaints, poor staff morale and a bad reputation. Those which train their staff thoroughly in all aspects of customer service, will be successful through increased sales, an enhanced reputation and a satisfied and confident workforce.

The principles of customer service

Why customer service is so important

In recent years customers have come to expect more from the products and services they are buying. What once may have been an added extra is now often a necessity. This is especially so in the travel and tourism industry. For example, en suite facilities in hotel bedrooms, new rides at theme parks, a drinks service on long coach journeys are now expected services and not extras.

Customer service also involves the way staff treat customers. Never ignore a customer or belittle them. How would you feel if you were treated in this way? Remember, the way you treat customers will have a major effect on how the customer views the organisation. Travel and tourism depends on customers, not the other way round.

It is important that a flexible customer service policy is developed by an organisation. In the past, customers had to take or leave the level of service offered. This is no longer the case. Travel and tourism is now far more diverse and there is intense competition between organisations for a limited number of customers. This means that staff and organisations have to be far more flexible. The aim is to have satisfied customers who will return with repeat business, so retaining the customer base. Potentially, satisfied customers also give an organisation a competitive advantage through personally recommending the organisation, as well as enhancing its image.

CASE STUDY

The Portland Hotel

Here are some of the customer service features that the Portland Hotel provides for its business guests.

- Guests who book on a regular basis are allocated their own car-parking space during their stay. This saves time and the pressure of driving round looking for somewhere to park.

- A monthly newsletter is sent out to regular guests giving details of new restaurants and what's on at the local theatre. This means that businesspeople can plan their time to relax after a hard day on the road.

- The hotel's administrative staff are available to deal with any business-related tasks the businessperson has to complete, for example sending faxes, emailing important information, word processing documents. This service is free of charge. Once again this saves time and eases pressure.

1 What do you think the Portland Hotel is trying to achieve by offering these extra services?
2 Do you think the benefits would justify the costs?

Making your business succeed

Travel and tourism organisations must recognise that their survival and continued success will depend on the way their customers are treated.

Customer service means putting customers first. Successful organisations make a point of putting their customers' needs at the heart of their policies and procedures.

Giving excellent customer service plays an important part in helping travel and tourism organisations keep their existing customers and attract new ones. This is brought about by people recommending to friends and relatives the organisation's products and services, and, just as important, the way they are treated.

Success comes in the form of increased sales, fewer complaints, satisfied customers and an enhanced reputation. The ultimate test of excellent customer service is the amount of repeat business an organisation generates, that is loyal customers returning on a regular basis.

Poor service is bad news! If you have ever received poor service in a restaurant, shop or hotel then the chances are you will not go back. You are more likely to go to their nearest competitor.

Poor service makes customers unhappy and creates a poor image of the company

Business surveys indicate that organisations lose customers for the following reasons:

* 1% die

* 3% move away

* 4% float from one organisation to another

* 7% change organisations on the recommendation of friends

* 9% change because they can buy more cheaply elsewhere

* 76% stop dealing with organisations because sales staff and others giving service are indifferent and show little interest in them or their needs.

Think about it

Imagine someone rings up a local coach operator asking for details about a weekend in London. The conversation goes something like this:

Customer: 'Good morning. Could you give me details of the three-day London special I saw advertised in the local newspaper?'

Receptionist: 'Ah well, that offer shouldn't have been put in the newspaper until next week. Besides, we've changed it now anyway. We have got another special in three weeks' time but that's all booked up. Anything else I can help you with?'

What might be the result of this situation?

Selling products and services

Income is generated by the sale of products and services. This means costs are covered and profits can be made.

The majority of selling in travel and tourism is made through face-to-face communication with the customer. The travel agent (the seller) tries to persuade the potential client (the customer) to buy a holiday, therefore knowledge of selling and sales techniques is essential in these situations. Sales techniques are discussed in more detail on page 80.

Effective selling skills contribute to customer satisfaction as customers can be provided with the products that suit their needs. This can lead to future business (repeat business) and can guarantee long-term success for the organisation due to this established business.

You may know people who have used the same travel agent for years. This doesn't happen by chance. Many travel and tourism organisations try to build up an almost family-type of atmosphere when developing relationships with customers.

Skills practice

Products don't sell themselves. It takes a good salesperson to sell the benefits of a product so that it proves attractive to the customer. He or she may close the sale by saying, ' I am sure you will love it there, it's got everything you want.' A less competent salesperson may say 'I think you will like it there', which doesn't sound very convincing.

Think about the times you have been buying things and answer the following questions.

* Did the salesperson persuade you that you needed the product?

* What actions by the salesperson either encouraged you to buy or put you off?

* Have you ever felt threatened by over-enthusiastic salespeople?

* How can salespeople avoid creating a threatening situation?

Key terms

Customer service This involves an organisation ensuring that customers are treated in the best possible way in the hope that they will buy the products and services of the organisation, continue to buy them and tell other people about how well they were treated.

After sales service After a sale is made, customer service continues in the form of dealing with complaints or contacting customers to find out if they were pleased with the level of service they received.

Increased sales and profitability

All travel and tourism organisations have to make profits, otherwise they would go out of business. The first contact a customer has with an organisation can be the deciding factor as to whether that customer buys the product or service on offer.

An organisation with an excellent reputation for looking after its customers and providing what they want, is usually able to increase its customer base through recommendation from its satisfied customers. This leads to increased sales and more profit that can be used to expand the organisation and thus offer more choice to customers.

Though the private and public sectors are different in that private industry aims to make a profit from its activities, the public sector organisations, like museums and tourist information centres, nevertheless adopt the same standard of customer service as those in the private sector. After all, they also want to increase usage.

The English Tourism Council has the following customer service policy aimed at providing customer satisfaction:

* Exceeding customers' expectations
* Making sure that every customer recommends us
* Putting the customer first and at the centre of everything.

These aims would help all organisations meet sales and profit targets.

Increased reputation

All travel and tourism organisations like to promote the fact that they have a good reputation and a good public image. This is a way of showing customers that the products on offer are good value for money and that the service they receive is second to none.

If an organisation has a positive image then customers will have more confidence in it. So if the organisation can improve and develop its reputation then it should be able to increase its sales and attract customers as more people become aware of what the organisation offers to those customers. Competition between travel and tourism organisations is fierce and if one organisation is able to offer better quality of service than a competitor it stands to get more business.

A good public image can be created by using endorsements from satisfied customers. This strengthens the image of the organisation by showing that the customers who use that organisation are happy with the service they have received and the products they have bought. Travel and tourism organisations also use photographs showing people enjoying themselves because they are using the organisation's products and services. The aim of this is to project a good image, encourage new custom and build up loyalty.

CASE STUDY

Increasing sales

Travel and tourism organisations have to make a profit in order to stay in business. Increased sales can lead to profits. However, survival is not the only aim, an organisation has to develop and expand so that new products and services can attract existing and potential customers.

A theme park, for example, aims to provide customers with fun, thrills, excitement and value for money. Customers either pay an entrance fee allowing them to go on any ride or buy tickets for individual rides.

1 How can the theme park encourage customers to return year after year?
2 What products and services can it offer so that ancillary or secondary sales, that is those that are additional to the main product, will increase?

Newark Tourist Information Centre provides a variety of services. Information about places to visit within the town is available to local people and overseas visitors.

The information it gives includes accommodation availability, restaurant prices, entertainment venues, antique fairs and tourist attractions. It also gives a five-day weather forecast.

The products it sells includes maps, souvenirs such as key rings, pens and posters.

Twice a year an undercover inspector posing as a customer assesses the quality of service given by the staff, who are judged on their performance in answering the phone, the response time to requests for information and general efficiency.

Last year the centre was voted the best in the region for customer service.

1 How has the Tourist Information Centre built up a first-class reputation?
2 What do we mean by the expression 'Reputations take a long time to build but can be lost overnight'?
3 How could the staff at Newark Tourist Information Centre be classed as salespeople?

A competitive edge

Organisations which care about their customers will try to provide high-quality service which gives them an edge over the competition. This can be achieved by providing a wider range of products, effective promotion and, most of all, higher standards of customer service. For example, this could be by anticipating customers' needs and offering extra services, such as a hotel which offers guests a choice of newspapers or an airport which offers a free bus service from the car park to the terminal buildings.

Many travel and tourism organisations offer similar products, for example all travel agents sell holidays and insurance, all hotels offer rooms, all airlines sell seats. In some cases, customers prefer to stay with the same travel and tourism organisation even though its products and services aren't as wide-ranging as others; it's the standard of customer service that attracts them!

Two coach operators in the Midlands specialise in day trips for senior citizens. Staff in both organisations are friendly and well trained and drivers are encouraged to build up a rapport with their passengers.

One of the coach operators picks up and drops off its passengers at their doorsteps. It also provides bingo, raffles and quizzes to help make the journeys more interesting and fun. It also gives each passenger a small gift on the return leg of the trip.

These three small extras give this coach operator the edge over its competitor.

How could the other coach operator improve its customer service to compete on the same level?

Customer satisfaction and repeat business

Nowadays customers expect more than just the basic product and will only use an organisation again if they feel confident in the type of service they have received. This in turn will lead to repeat business, increasing sales even further.

Satisfied customers are those who are satisfied with the products and services they have paid for and the way they have been treated. They are also satisfied because they have

* received value for money
* been treated with respect
* had their needs fulfilled.

For example, a family group may have paid £5000 for a holiday in Florida. At the airport they were met by the organisation's representative and were transferred to their resort in an air-conditioned coach. The hotel was clean and near to all the attractions, including the beach.

A babysitting service was provided for the children and a free taxi was provided for mum and dad so that they could have a few drinks in the nearby restaurant, knowing they didn't have to drive back.

Going-away gifts were presented to the children on the last day and the holiday rep stayed at the airport with them to ensure they boarded their plane on time.

Travel and tourism organisations must meet customers' needs and expectations. To achieve this they must be committed to providing the highest standards of customer service and therefore must

* develop the right mix of products and services
* ensure high-quality delivery

Travel and tourism organisations must provide the right mix of products and services for customers

* measure customer satisfaction
* train staff in customer service.

Never underestimate the importance of providing customer satisfaction and always recognise the danger of leaving customers dissatisfied!

Key terms

Competitive edge This is when organisations strive to achieve an advantage over the competition, in being better than they are at providing products and services. This could be achieved by better customer service, providing a wider range of products or giving better value for money.

Repeat business Customers who are happy with the service and the products they have received from an organisation usually return for more of the same because they are satisfied with the way they have been treated.

Value for money This is when customers feel satisfied with the products they have bought and believe their money has been well spent.

Skills practice

People tend to be creatures of habit. Once they find something they enjoy they will tend to stay with it. Eighty per cent of business in the travel and tourism industry comes from regular customers, so it makes good business sense to ensure that their visit or experience is as good as, if not better than, the last one. Likewise, unhappy customers will tell between ten and fifteen people about their experience.

Answer the following questions on the value of customer satisfaction and repeat business:

1 What are the benefits of having a loyal customer base?

2 How does this reduce advertising costs?

3 What effect does repeat business have on staff?

First impressions are lasting impressions

Providing a warm welcome for customers means going beyond basic manners and politeness. It is being willing to go 'the extra mile'. This is what

The first impression you make on a customer is crucial to being successful

makes a true, professional customer service employee stand out.

Customers notice almost immediately how clean and tidy any facility is kept, whether it is a hotel reception or even the inside of a plane. Who would want to spend ten hours on a flight with litter on the floor and the remnants of someone's meal on their seat? What state would the toilets be in on such a flight?

Customers also notice whether the person dealing with them is neat, clean and well groomed, and whether that person is working in an efficient and orderly manner. For example, is the travel consultant wearing a smart uniform? Do they answer the phone in the correct way? Do they make eye contact with the person they are dealing with?

Customers will not only make a judgement about the person attending them and about how well they are meeting their needs, they will also make a judgement about the organisation that person is representing.

Research has shown that first impressions are formed within seven seconds and embedded within thirty seconds, and it is almost impossible to change a customer's opinion if the initial contact has not been positive. In short, first impressions are lasting impressions. The implications of this are that customers will no buy products and services from an organisation which does not immediately impress them either because of their staff or the environment.

> **Key term**
>
> **First impressions** This is the image presented by staff of the facility itself that immediately decides whether or not a customer likes what he or she sees, which is why it is vital to make an excellent first impresison.

CASE STUDY

First impressions

The Regional Manager of a well-known travel agency states 'We encourage our staff to create a really positive impression. Their uniforms are extremely smart and everyone wears a polished name badge . . . along with a big smile.'

He goes on to say that staff are able to put customers at ease and are able to listen to and understand the needs of their customers.

1 **What rules regarding dress code would you put in place for your staff?**
2 **How would you know if your staff were creating a favourable impression?**

Uniforms and dress code

Many travel and tourism organisations provide staff with uniforms. You have only to look at travel agency staff or air cabin crew to see how smart they look. Among the advantages of providing staff with uniforms are that they

* are functional
* present a professional image
* make it easy to recognise staff as being part of the organisation
* give staff a sense of belonging to a team and so loyalty is also promoted.

There are usually certain codes that organisations insist on. For example, men are not allowed to wear earrings, their hair must be tidy and smart, beards and moustaches are not allowed, and tattoos must not be visible. In the case of women, make-up should be conventional and not excessive

A dress code creates a professional image

Clothes not only say a lot about you personally, they also say something about the organisation. Basic rules should apply to appearance, for example clothes should be clean and ironed and appropriate to the role. For example, 'T' shirts are not acceptable in business situations, even if they are the latest designer fashion costing over £60!

Skills practice

Customers judge staff and therefore the organisation for which they work by the way they look and act, that is their appearance and attitude.

As the manager of a travel agency you have noticed recently that one of your travel consultants has started to come in looking a little unkempt and haggard.

1 How would you handle this situation?

2 Why would you have to deal with it as a priority?

You could act this out with a colleague.

Attitude and behaviour

The expression 'Your attitude is showing' means that you can't hide how you are feeling. That is why it is always wise to adopt a positive approach to work.

Your behaviour will have a profound effect on customers. No one can actually see your thoughts and feelings, they can only see how you behave and what you say, and this is what customers base their impressions of you, and your organisation, on.

In travel and tourism staff are providing services to other people, so the attitude adopted by them towards customers could make the difference between people returning to buy the product or not. Having a positive attitude is made up of believing in yourself, taking pride and belief in your organisation and having respect for the customer. Someone who believes in the values and aims of their organisation will be enthusiastic towards customers, whereas someone who is critical of their organisation can have a damaging effect.

Respect for the customer has to be genuine – you can't fake sincerity! Training can help instil this respect, however staff must have a natural, genuine interest in people if they are to offer the right level of customer service. Take, for example, a receptionist who has dealt with hundreds of customers at a theme park in the first hour of opening. An enthusiastic receptionist may feel tired but doesn't show it. She has told herself to treat every customer as if they were the first. This is thinking positive.

Take the trouble to project a belief in yourself and adopt a positive attitude. This can make you feel good about yourself and others. This approach willl certainly be appreciated by customers.

Your behaviour is like a beacon, sending out signals to all the people with whom you have dealings. The signals you send out are vital because they are a major influence on the reactions of the customer. They can either help or hinder any transaction you make with them. Remember, enthusiasm and a positive attitude enable you to build up relationships with customers quite quickly. On the other hand, misery spreads!

Skills practice

Having a positive mental attitude enables you to tackle problems or situations you wouldn't have thought possible. By adopting a positive mental attitude, how would you handle the following situations:

1 You have to tell a group of passengers their flight has been delayed for twelve hours.

2 A family of four has to move hotel due to a double booking.

3 There are rumours of redundancies being made at your organisation.

Discuss with another student or as a class.

**Think positive!
Act positive!
Be positive!**

Travel Assistant

Think about it

Even the most professional employee can sometimes feel less than enthusiastic towards customers. This could be the result of lack of sleep or even a hangover. The latter could be reflected in the smell of alcohol on your breath or the smell of stale cigarettes on your clothes. It is one thing to try and disguise the way you feel; it is a bigger challenge to disguise the way you look.

How do you think customers would react to the above situation?

Recognising customer needs

The needs of customers are an important consideration for all travel and tourism

organisations because they have a direct bearing on the demand for products and services. According to Maslow (1943), people's needs must be satisfied in some hierarchical order, starting first with physical needs then followed by social and psychological needs.

Maslow believed that the order of the levels of need were important. As needs at level 1 are satisfied, so those on the next level become more dominant, and so on.

Self-fulfilment

Esteem

Social needs

Safety needs

Physiological needs

Figure 2.2 Maslow's pyramid of needs

These needs can be related to a travel and tourism product such as a holiday:

* Physiological needs — warmth, food, drink, sleep

* Safety needs — secure environment, safe destination

* Social needs — belonging, socialising, making new friends

* Esteem — status, travelling first class

* Self-fulfilment — learning a new skill, for example paragliding, surfing

Think about it

After the physiological needs have been met, the second need of customers is safety. Customers will want to make sure that equipment checks have been carried out when they take part in high-risk activities on holiday, such as paragliding, water-skiing or bungee jumping. They also want to know if staff are trained and qualified when they take part in sports like sub-aqua diving.

Imagine you are on holiday in Spain and have the opportunity to take part in relatively high-risk sports activities. In terms of safety, what would be the order of priority of your needs?

Most people have wants but they cannot afford to satisfy them. However, when you have the money to back up your desires, wants become demands which, in the travel and tourism industry, can be expressed in many ways, such as the number of overseas holidays taken or the amount spent on tourist attractions in a year.

A person's needs will vary with age and family circumstances and will affect demand for travel and tourism products and services. It is therefore vital that customer needs are recognised and met accordingly.

The specific needs of travel and tourism customers cover many areas including the following.

Products

Market research is conducted to find out what customers are looking for. If you don't give people what they want you are not providing good customer service and they will go elsewhere. For example, a couple on honeymoon may want secluded beaches on a paradise island, whereas a family group may want a self-catering holiday in Crete. Providing the right product to the right people is fundamentally important in customer service.

CASE STUDY
Identifying underlying needs

A young man walks into a restaurant to book a table for two. What he actually wants to do is to propose to his girlfriend in a romantic setting.

1   As the restaurant manager how could you find out exactly what your customer's needs are?

2   How could you fulfil them?

Help

Customers usually look to travel and tourism staff for practical help, such as the directions to the nearest restaurant or carrying a guest's luggage from the taxi to the hotel.

Advice

Customers ask for advice because they want to be sure that the activities they want to take part in are suitable and safe, for example asking if a particular theme park ride is suitable for children or asking a travel consultant about the different types of insurance.

Think about it

An American backpacker walks into a tourist information centre wanting to know about cheap, local accommodation near to the railway station so that he can catch the early morning train to London.

It would be irresponsible of the receptionist to say something like, 'If you look in Yellow Pages you might find what you are looking for.'

The correct procedure would be for the receptionist to phone a bed and breakfast nearest to the station and book it for him.

What other information could the receptionist give to the American visitor?

Information

Customers may need information because they are unfamiliar with a place. Travel and tourism staff need to know how to give this information, either by face-to-face communication or in the form of brochures and leaflets. The information customers may require could range from 'What type of visa will I need for visiting South Africa?' to 'What time does the park close?'.

Safety and security

Ensuring customer safety and security is a vitally important part of customer service. Customers need to know that they and others with them will be safe. This is why airports check luggage, why safety deposit boxes for passports and valuables are available at hotels, why fire exits are kept clear, why theme park rides are checked regularly. All these procedures are carried out to give customers peace of mind.

To be understood

This need can be fulfilled by staff who listen carefully to what customers need and can empathise with their situation. For example, holidaymakers looking for peace and quiet don't want nightclub music blasting out until all hours of the morning. They didn't pay £3000 for that. In this case a transfer to another, more peaceful hotel would seem appropriate.

Made to feel welcome

When people arrive at a new place for the first time they are often anxious about fitting in and meeting other people. Travel and tourism staff should be aware of this and act as good hosts. A friendly greeting and a warm smile makes customers feel welcome. This in turn makes them more relaxed and gives them confidence in the staff charged with looking after them.

Feeling important

One way of making people feel important is to call them by their name. 'Good morning Miss Beadle, how are you today?' sounds a lot better than a plain 'Good morning' or even 'Good morning madam'. People like to be recognised and called by their name; it makes them feel important and wanted. Customers have every right to feel important, especially if they have spent a lot of money on the organisation's products and services.

Think about it

If someone calls you by your name it makes you feel important and you appreciate that they have taken the trouble to find it out.

How could you find out a customer's name in advance so that when you greeted them you could use their name?

Feeling comfortable

A warm, friendly environment puts people at their ease and gives them a sense of comfort and security. This may be fulfilled when all other needs have been taken care of.

The aim of meeting customers' needs is to provide customer satisfaction. It is therefore imperative to recognise and fulfil these needs, given that the success of the business will be affected by the recommendations of satisfied customers.

People working in travel and tourism have to be thoroughly trained to recognise and satisfy customers' needs. The organisations themselves need to invest heavily in customer service training so that the employees know how to treat and look after customers properly. Making such an investment should pay off in terms of increased sales and satisfied customers.

CASE STUDY
Meeting needs is no accident

Ricky Aston was, at twenty-seven, one of the youngest hotel managers in London. The guests of his hotel included foreign politicians, pop stars, celebrities and even royalty.

Naturally these sorts of guests have particular needs. Ricky found it very exciting but at times quite daunting dealing with some of the guests. There were things that had to be handled with extreme sensitivity, like security or television interviews and press conferences. Ricky seemed to be able to take these in his stride.

He started his career in a small Brighton hotel and studied part-time for a Diploma in Management. After two years he was promoted to assistant manager in charge of twenty staff.

Further part-time study in Hospitality Management followed. This was extremely challenging as he had to attend college three hours every Monday evening, complete ten

hours coursework each week and hold down a full-time job which included shift work. He fulfilled one of his ambitions at the age of twenty-three when he became deputy manager of a top London hotel. Four years later he was promoted to his present position.

A combination of study, training and experience had enabled Ricky to manage staff effectively and recognise and satisfy customers' needs as a top priority.

1 **What skills and qualities do you think you need to reach the top of your chosen profession?**
2 **What sort of on-the-job training would Ricky have received?**
3 **What topics would have been included in Ricky's studies?**

The needs of external customers

External customers are those outside the organisations of the travel and tourism industry who are purchasing the products and services of those organisations: visitors, clients, guests, the public. All of them have needs which they satisfy by purchasing products and services from organisations, and they must be given the best customer service possible as they expect value for money and will recommend any organisation that provides it, which will contribute to the success of the business.

Satisfying customer needs is vital to the success of an organisation, as are the following points employees are trained to bear in mind when dealing with customers, namely that customers

* are always right
* pay our wages
* are the main purpose of our job
* are not to be argued with
* are people with feelings and needs, not statistics
* trust our expertise to give them what they want.

The following is used by many travel and tourism organisations as a reminder of the importance of customers.

Rule 1 The customer is always right
Rule 2 If the customer is ever wrong, re-read rule 1!!!

Key terms

Customer charter A document produced by an organisation that sets out the minumum levels of service and standards that customers should receive when they use the organisation.

External customers People from outside the organisation who pay for the organisation's products and services.

Skills practice

The two rules above were written by an American entrepreneur. Other expressions include 'The customer is King' and 'No customers, no business'.

Working alone or with another student, devise three expressions which show the importance of customers and how they are looked after.

Customers are treated as individuals, however they can also be identified and treated as groups of individuals sharing certain characteristics. This applies to any organisation in the service sector. To identify the special needs of groups of people enables an organisation to make sure it provides the products and services that meet the needs of the individuals in those groups.

The following are the sorts of groups of customers the travel and tourism industry has to provide products and services for:

✴ Other organisations in the travel and tourism industry, e.g. coach operators who would be seen as customers of a theme park

✴ People of different ages

✴ People from different cultural backgrounds

✴ People with specific needs.

It isn't easy to provide high customer service to a wide range of customers with different needs. To succeed staff need to be appropriately trained to do the job, enthusiastic, committed and hard working.

Obviously there are times when the customer is not always right. They may have misinterpreted information or possibly have been told by friends that they were entitled to certain discounts when in fact they didn't fall into that particular category. These situations have to be dealt with sensitively and with tact. This is dealt with in more detail on page 83.

Individuals

An organisation may only have to satisfy the needs of one person who wishes to buy the products and services of that organisation. Having to satisfy only one person's needs can simplify the task. However some individuals can be a problem, making awkward requests or being demanding just for the sake of it. If you are faced with such a customer and feel isolated or exposed, always seek support from your manager. Remember, asking for support is a strength, not a weakness.

In dealing with individual customers try to find out their name and use it. This is one way you can make the customer feel important and at ease, and make it easier for you to deal with them. 'Good morning Mr White, good to see you again' is one way of making a customer feel good and putting them at ease.

Individual customers may feel awkward when visiting a travel agent, for example, so the staff should make a special effort to make the customer feel relaxed and at ease. A warm welcome from a well-presented, friendly member of staff goes a long way to putting someone at ease.

CASE STUDY
Putting people at ease

Some people are excellent at making customers feel welcome and relaxed. It seems to come naturally to them. They tend to be staff who are genuinely interested in customers and can build up a rapport in minutes.

Some young people may feel shy when talking to older people. Perhaps they feel older people may be intimidated by young people.

You will probably find that gradual exposure to customer service will build up your own confidence as you develop your customer service skills.

Many people believe you have to be an extrovert to work in the travel and tourism industry and be blessed with a sparkling personality. This is not so. Anyone with a pleasant personality who is capable of listening can succeed.

1 How would you rate yourself as someone who could provide excellent customer service?
2 How would you deal with a customer who came into your travel agency looking extremely unsure of himself, ready to bolt to the nearest exit?

Customers have basic needs: to be understood, to feel comfortable, to feel welcome, to feel important. So how do you find out an individual's needs? It is quite easy, really. Use an open question like 'How may I help you?' Asking questions increases the possibility of the customer doing the talking.

The following are examples of the needs of an individual that need to be satisfied by a travel and tourism organisation:

* A businessperson staying at a hotel wants the *Daily Telegraph* left outside their bedroom door each morning. This is because he may have a breakfast meeting or an early morning business meeting and needs to gather the latest financial news.

* A customer in a travel agency may want an adventure holiday. This is because they have been on holiday to the usual places but now want to go trekking in the Himalayas to fulfil their spirit of adventure.

Whatever the circumstances, it is vital that travel and tourism organisations recognise the needs of customers and provide for their needs.

Groups

A group is a number of people who want to take part in the same activity. For example, holidaymakers gathered together to listen to the travel representative's talk would be classed as a group. The advantage of dealing with groups of customers is that it can save time, as it is possible to deal with several customers at once. This means that groups are good for business. Every group booking involves less sales time and reduced staff time. One advantage for the customer is that group bookings often attract discounts.

However, travel and tourism staff must realise that although groups might be made up of families, young couples, senior citizens and people holidaying alone, each group member has to be treated as an individual.

It requires special skills to take into account the needs of individual customers while dealing with the group as a whole. Groups can be disruptive or threatening to individual customers, if only through the sheer numbers in the group, for example a coach load of football fans spilling into a pub.

Group members can also become angry and frustrated if their visit is not managed well, as in the case of having to queue up for thirty minutes to collect tickets you paid for the previous day.

There are several ways of managing groups which may help avoid irritation. These include:

* A separate entrance for groups to allow speedy access

* Advance booking – reduces bottlenecks at entry

* Identifiable guide to sort out the problem

* Re-emphasising group benefits – discounts on admission, priority bookings for the future.

Information for the group is usually communicated by the leader, for example a holiday representative or tour guide. It can be quite daunting for most people to stand up and speak to twenty or more people. However, these reps are fully trained and exude a confidence that wins over most groups. The situation needs someone who can raise their voice, make the information sound interesting and keep the group within earshot and eye contact. You also need to catch and keep people's attention.

Managing groups can be made easier if

* their needs are met fully

* group members are recognised as individuals and not numbers

* they have a leader in whom they have confidence.

Skills practice

As a holiday rep in Malia in Crete you have to organise the day and evening activities for your group of 18–30-year-olds. What's more, you somehow have to keep them 'under control' so that they don't interfere with anyone else's enjoyment. The programme of events includes a beach party in the afternoon followed by a 'Pirates of the Caribbean' evening.

Together with another student answer these questions:

1 How would you go about organising these events?

2 How would you ensure your party received value for money?

3 How would you manage the group – all fifty of them?

People of different ages

Staff who work in the travel and tourism industry have to communicate with people of widely differing ages. Age affects people's behaviour and needs. Customer age groups can be classified as children – from babies to teenagers – and adults – from young adults to senior citizens.

A group of customers may consist of adults with young children or parents with grandchildren, a combination of ages. This means that travel and tourism staff will need to identify and satisfy the specific needs of each age group. For example, a family group on holiday may look like this: gran and granddad want to relax by the pool; mum and dad want to go to the beach; the children want to join in the organised games.

> ## CASE STUDY
> ### Holiday differences
> Holidays are supposed to be occasions when you can relax and do whatever you like. The pressures of work have been forgotten and it is now time to busily employ yourself in rest and relaxation.
>
> Sometimes there are obstacles preventing this taking place, especially when the occasion involves a family group consisting of people of different ages who have different needs.
>
> **Identify the needs of the different people in this family group and come up with ideas to meet their needs: grandma and granddad; mum and dad; Sue aged 17; Josh aged 13; twins Sarah and Jack aged four.**

Let's look at the different age categories in more detail and identify their needs.

Under-fives

Many travel and tourism organisations promote specific services and facilities for babies and toddlers. This is a way of encouraging parents to visit a destination because they know the needs of their youngsters will be met.

The under-five age group's needs can be met by providing child-friendly facilities such as baby changing rooms, special family areas in restaurants, play areas and a crèche. Airlines may provide a 'sky cot' and jars of food for babies.

Good customer service provides alternative options for children while adults follow their own pursuits. For older children and teenagers a variety of exciting, safe activities can be provided by travel and tourism organisations, especially during family holidays. These include ten-pin bowling, paintballing, laserquest, go-karting, karaoke competitions and of course having fast-food meals.

Young adults

This age group also has its particular set of needs. Tour operators organise holidays specifically for 18–30-year-olds consisting of activities like beach parties and barbecues, themed evenings and fancy dress parties. The main aim is to provide fun, excitement, opportunities for socialising and romance so that everyone can concentrate on having a good time.

Older people

Travel and tourism organisations now recognise that people over sixty years of age have spending power, and tour operators such as Saga target this particular age group, in fact they target the fifty-plus market.

Demographic factors concerning the age structure of the population influence the travel and tourism industry. For example, there is an increasing number of older people in the UK, due to the increase in life expectancy because of improved levels of healthcare and advances in medicine, which is pushing back the definition of the 'elderly'. As a result there is a new market for products and services in travel and tourism for the older customer as their disposable income increases along with better pension schemes.

The number of over sixty-five-year-olds is forecast to grow. This should be looked on as a positive trend for the travel and tourism industry because many potential customers in this age group have paid off their mortgages and no longer have children to support. This 'grey' market has time and money to spend on leisure pursuits like holidays. In Australia this age group is known as 'Grey Nomads', such is their love of travel.

Traditional stereotypes do not apply any more when it comes to older people. It is not unheard of for people of sixty years plus to go trekking in the Himalayas. Obviously some older customers do have requirements traditionally associated with their age, like mobility, hard of hearing or poor sight problems.

As in the case of all customers, a level of respect and patience is required when dealing with older people, although travel and tourism employees should not make assumptions about someone's needs based solely on their age. They should judge each customer's case individually.

Skills practice

It is tempting and convenient to stereotype older people as being inactive and dependent on others. This is an untrue generalisation.

Answer the following questions, conducting research wherever necessary:

1 What sort of things do older people look for in a holiday?

2 In what ways do you think your age group is stereotyped?

3 How do you think older people are stereotyped?

4 Think about the older people you know. What do they like to do in their leisure time?

Customers from different cultural backgrounds

Culture is associated with people's tastes, traditions and way of life. It is important to understand someone's cultural background so that they can be provided with the most effective type of customer service. Customers from different cultures may still speak English but have different ways of doing things. You may have experienced different cultures when you have been abroad on holiday and you may experience cultural differences in your own country which include diet, language and dress.

Cultural differences can include handshakes and body language. For example, making a circle with the forefinger and thumb in the UK means everything is OK. However in Brazil it is classed as a very rude gesture.

HSBC bank promotes itself as 'The world's local' bank. Its advertisements show people in different countries adopting different habits to us. For example, showing the soles of your feet in Thailand is extremely rude or eating all your food in Japan is a sign that you are not fully satisfied with the food provided. HSBC's message is quite simple: people in different countries have different ways of doing things and HSBC recognises these needs through the way they treat their customers.

Skills practice

Many people in the UK expect everyone to speak English when they go abroad. In the same way, many of us expect overseas visitors to speak fluent English when they come to the UK. Obviously this is not always the case.

Answer the following questions:

1 How would you prepare yourself for receiving customers who do not speak English?

2 How would you prepare your workplace, for example a hotel, for non-English speaking guests?

A question asked is 'How can travel and tourism employees recognise cultural differences?' Air cabin crew and holiday representatives are encouraged to do this through reading, talking to friends and colleagues from other cultures or experiencing the culture themselves by spending time in that country.

As with other aspects of customer service, dealing with customers from different cultures is not simply a case of being nice. It takes training and practice. This can help reduce any misunderstandings and should ensure that customers from different cultures are treated properly and that all their needs are met.

Customers with specific needs

All customers have their own special needs and wants. Some customers have more specific needs and require extra understanding and sensitive treatment. These include people needing wheelchair access, those with sensory disabilities and people with young children.

When they recognise that customers have specific needs, travel and tourism staff should choose an appropriate means of communication, either spoken or written, or think about any special information the customers need, such as disabled facilities.

> **Skills practice**
>
> The Disability Discrimination Act 1995 covers customer service for people with disabilities or specific needs. Facilities now have to ensure that people with disabilities are able to access and have the opportunity to take part in activities like anyone else. For example, theme parks will need to provide adapted seats on rides for people with disabilities.
>
> Carry out research into the Act in order to answer the following question.
>
> What provisions for specific needs do you think other travel and tourism organisations will have to make in order to comply with this legislation?

Of course we should see customers as people with particular needs, not as difficult people. People with specific needs want the same level of service that every customer receives, with possibly a little more understanding. Visitors with restricted mobility include those in wheelchairs to those who have stiff joints. It also includes people who are temporarily disabled through, for example, breaking a leg.

Not all travel and tourism facilities are ideally constructed or equipped to deal with this type of disability. The situation can be helped by considering the following points:

✱ Is there enough space for them to sit/stand/move/manoeuvre?

✱ Is there a shorter route they can take with fewer obstacles/changes of level?

✱ Can they reach handles, controls, shelves, and telephones or will they need help?

✱ Will they need help to carry things, or open doors if they are on crutches, for example?

✱ Do you need to slow down if you are guiding them somewhere?

Visually-impaired visitors

Many people have some form of visual impairment, but only a small proportion are totally blind and some only experience lack of colour definition. Information in large print format or printed text in Braille can be useful. The following points could be considered.

✱ When guiding a blind person, ask how they would like you to guide them. Most prefer you to walk slightly ahead while they take your arm.

✱ Explain exactly what obstacles are ahead, for example a set of stairs going up.

✱ Avoid intrusive background noise, such as loud piped music – blind people rely more on hearing their way than sighted people.

✱ When introducing yourself to a blind person who does not recognise your voice, tell them who you are, and address them by their name if you know it.

Hearing-impaired visitors

Again the nature of disability varies from person to person. The following points may aid communication.

* Face the person on the same level, with your face to the light and not in front of a bright window.

* Keep your hands or pen away from your face and do not eat whilst speaking.

* Check that background noise is kept to a minimum.

* Make sure the hearing impaired person is looking at you – attract their attention if necessary.

* If the topic of conversation is changed, make sure the hearing-impaired person knows.

* Speak the words clearly, maintaining a normal rhythm of speech.

* Do not shout as it distorts the visual effect of words.

* Use visual material and gestures where it helps understanding, but avoid exaggerated or inappropriate facial expressions.

* Remember that phrases and sentences are easier to understand than isolated words.

* If a word/phrase is not understood, use different words with the same meaning rephrased.

* Allow more time for the person to absorb what you are saying.

* Remember that lip reading can be very tiring.

It is important to remember that a person is not disabled by their impairment but by the environment and attitudes of the people they encounter.

People with young children

People with specific needs also include customers with young children who may be restricted by the needs of the children.

In the example of a theme park, these needs can be met by providing breastfeeding and crèche facilities, baby-changing rooms, special family areas in the catering areas and use of free pushchairs.

All customers have needs and expectations, some more than others. Travel and tourism staff have to recognise this needs something which can only usually be achieved by thorough training and experience. It is not easy to satisfy all customer needs but practice and experience will help you deal effectively with all customer service requirements. In time, your confidence and experience will grow.

The needs of internal customers

Internal customers are employees who work in different sections or departments of an organisation. Everyone in a travel and tourism organisation must work well together so that the organisation can give excellent customer service.

Internal customers may also include other organisations such as catering franchises operating in a theme park. At the same time, organisations must treat the internal customers to the same degree as their external customers in order to get the best out of them and establish good working relations between colleagues, managers and staff teams.

It might at first seem strange to think of your colleagues as customers, but you have the same responsibility to each other as you have to external customers.

Good levels of communication between different departments are required to ensure that travel and tourism organisations operate smoothly to meet the needs of external customers. For example, imagine you work in a travel agency. We know that your external customers are the people who want to book a holiday or arrange travel insurance. To reach that stage in the transaction, head office would have provided you with the posters to advertise the holidays, the computer systems to enable you to make a reservation and the skills you need to operate the computers.

In this case, you are the internal customer because you need the product. Your requests have been communicated to the departments and they have responded positively so that the external customers' needs are fulfilled. If organisations

Employees of a company are internal customers

treat staff well it eventually reflects on the level of service that is delivered to customers. A happy and efficient workforce who provide good service to each other is more likely to provide good customer service to external customers.

It can take a while to get used to the idea of regarding your colleagues at work as customers. However, it must be emphasised that staff who come into direct contact with customers cannot provide them with excellent customer service unless they receive the same type of service and support from colleagues.

In many travel and tourism organisations, employees work in teams and members of these teams work together to deliver high-quality customer service.

People who work well together usually enjoy their work more. A happy workforce leads to good teamwork and greater efficiency. Job satisfaction leads to greater motivation and leads to a sense of pride in the organisation, an increase in self-confidence and the motivation to continue to do well.

People who can work well with others tend to be able to motivate them. This is especially useful in supervisory and management positions. Providing excellent internal customer service will not only improve external customer service but can result in co-operation from colleagues, recognition from management and improved chances of promotion.

Key terms

Internal customers These are the people who work within the same organisation as colleagues, who should support each other and co-operate with each other in order for the organisation to be a success. An internal customer should be given the same respect as an external customer.

Job satisfaction This is the degree to which employees enjoy their work and feel motivated to do it well.

The significance of induction and training

Induction is concerned with providing a new member of staff of an organisation with a structured introduction to the organisation and its employees.

An induction programme will help them become familiar with their duties and responsibilities. This will help them deliver effective customer service. The programme should be designed to help new members of staff familiarise themselves with their new work environment, settle into their new jobs and establish good working relations with other members of staff.

Starting a new job can be quite a daunting experience. In fact it can be very stressful and nerve-racking. A good induction programme should aim to make the new employee feel relaxed yet motivated about his/her new workplace.

Some organisations appoint an existing member of staff to assist the new employee to settle into their new surroundings. This is called mentoring. The mentor plays an important role in the induction process in that he/she can motivate and enthuse the new employee into working for an organisation that looks after its employees both during their induction and throughout their career.

Skills practice

Studying for qualifications and training to learn new skills will play a major part in your career progression. Your studies could include working towards certificates, diplomas or degrees. Your training could include using information technology, marketing and management.

You will need to do research to carry out the following:

1 Make a list of the courses which would be applicable to you if you were to continue your studies in travel and tourism.

2 What skills and qualifications would you need to become: a cabin crew manager; a travel consultant; a regional manager for holiday resort reps?

Recruiting a new employee is a big investment. A structured and well thought out induction programme will help ensure this investment pays dividends.

Many travel and tourism organisations provide their employees with some form of manual or booklet outlining the structure of their new organisation and including a number of important points of information, including health and safety, first aid, disciplinary procedures, as well as details about social clubs, pension arrangements and trade union membership.

The following example of an induction checklist shows what the new employee can expect during the first month in their new job.

Sherwood Health Club

Induction for Leisure Assistants

Name _____

Date _____

First day activities:
- Tour of club
- Introduction to staff
- Evacuation procedures
- Staff room and locker key issue
- Issue of staff uniform and name badge
- Staff handbook and club procedures booklet issued

First week activities:
- Shift rotas
- Pension schemes
- Annual leave
- Sickness procedures
- 'Shadowing' supervisor

Additional aspects to be covered:
- Organisational structure
- Career prospects
- Training programmes
- Community links
- Competition

Signed.................................... Manager

Signed.................................... Leisure Assistant

Date...

A good induction programme will ensure that new employees feel they have a valued part to play in their new organisation and should motivate them to want to do the very best for their new employer.

Imagine you work in the Human Resource department of Thomas Cook and are responsible for the induction programmes for all new trainee travel consultants. Work out an induction programme for them which would include their first day at work until they have finished their one year probationary period.

Many travel and tourism organisations, such as theme parks and tourist attractions like Blackpool Pleasure Beach, employ seasonal and part-time staff. It is just as important to provide a full induction programme to these staff as it is to full-time staff because they still have to look after customers, carry out any emergency procedures and know the layout of the organisation. Imagine on your first day at Alton Towers being told to operate 'Oblivion'! You may be inclined to ask, 'How'? 'Where is it'?' What happens if it breaks down'? 'Who will be my supervisor'?

This situation would never happen at Alton Towers, which is well known for giving excellent staff induction programmes followed up by additional training.

It is important to make sure all new staff are aware of their responsibilities towards customers. This is especially so when a large number of staff are starting their employment at the same time. In such cases travel and tourism organisations organise group induction sessions. This saves time and money and helps build teamwork right from the start as newcomers can get to know each other before they start their jobs.

CASE STUDY

A question of communication

Rio Fourget was staying with a friend in London for six months. He applied for a job in a restaurant by letter saying that he had worked as a kitchen hand and then as a waiter in a busy restaurant overseas.

To his surprise he received a letter back within three days asking him to come to the restaurant and be ready to start that day as the restaurant was very short of staff.

Rio turned up on time, looked extremely smart and was asked to start work in the café bar. Everything looked perfect. The manager came down to observe this very smart, friendly looking new member of staff. He was about to congratulate his assistant manager on this latest appointment when they discovered all was not well. They watched together as Rio took his first order. The customer seemed to be talking for quite a while, repeating his order. Was Rio hard of hearing? Was the customer a foreign visitor with limited English? The answer to both of these was a definite No! It was Rio who couldn't speak a word of English!

It is highly unlikely that a situation like this would ever occur. However it highlights the importance of ensuring the right procedures are followed to employ the right staff.

1 **What process should be followed when recruiting and selecting staff to work in travel and tourism?**
2 **What questions would you ask at an interview of someone wanting to be an air cabin crew member?**
3 **It is often said that interviewing is a skill. Why is that?**

Inductions should be made as interesting and motivating as possible. This helps create a positive first impression of the organisation for new staff as well as giving the impression of efficiency and careful planning.

Effective induction programmes should include guided tours, videos showing details of the organisation, team-building exercises and activities to 'break the ice' between new and existing employees. This helps get people talking and getting to know exactly what is involved in the job they have just taken on.

On-going training

Training should start on day one. A well-trained workforce will be productive because training will improve their knowledge of the job. They will also be more motivated, as people enjoy what they are doing if they know they are good at it.

Many travel and tourism organisations provide staff with on-going customer service training.

Customer service includes all contact with the customer whether it is face-to-face or dealing with letters of complaint. Travel and tourism organisations should provide quality training before allowing staff to deal with the public. It should be emphasised to staff during training that good customer service is one of the main aims of the organisation. Role-play situations are introduced so that new staff either play the part of a customer or play the part of sales staff. This gives them a good idea of what it is like in real life to be a customer on the receiving end of both good and bad service.

Types of training

After staff have gone through induction training there are ways they can improve their skills by taking additional training.

The first type of training is *on-the-job training*, which is basically learning by doing. This is the most common type of training and involves the employee learning how to do the job better by being shown how to do it, and then practising. It is also known as internal training.

The advantage of this type of training is that it is cost-effective for the employer in that the employee continues to work while learning. There is, however, one disadvantage. An experienced work colleague often carries out the internal training, so bad practices can be passed on to the new member of staff.

Another type of training is called *off-the-job training*, through which an employee learns away from their workplace, although on some occasions the training is still carried out internally if the organisation has a separate training division.

Off-the-job or external training often takes place at college. It can be more expensive than on-the-job training but it is often of a higher quality because better-qualified people teach it. This type of training is best used when introducing new skills or training people for promotion. Training will help with employees' personal development and enable them to take additional responsibilities.

The travel and tourism industry is highly competitive and every organisation must constantly be looking to improve and update to remain competitive. All organisations should aim to maximise the potential of each employee. This development benefits the person and the organisation.

The result of a planned professional development programme is that the employee is able to complete their job as effectively as possible.

The significance of product knowledge

Customers are likely to ask a range of questions relating to the products and services provided by an organisation. In order to sell its products, staff need to have a wide knowledge of the products and services offered by the organisation. This means that staff can answer specific questions or queries that may arise and can quickly and efficiently deal with problems.

Product knowledge is an essential requirement of a successful sales process. Staff working in travel and tourism must have regular training to help them learn about the features and benefits of the products they are selling. Good product knowledge creates the impression of a professional organisation as staff can suggest alternatives if a customer's first choice of product is not available, or provide in-depth information on the range of products available.

In the travel and tourism industry product knowledge is sometimes gained by staff experiencing the products first hand, for example familiarisation trips for travel consultants. Sometimes it is not always easy to obtain a working level of product knowledge, particularly when you first start a new job, but it is important that you take every opportunity to gain as much information as possible. In many cases, work colleagues are usually helpful in providing the relevant information.

So that travel and tourism staff can give information and advice about products, they need to know about

* the range of products available, for example holidays, rooms available, flight times

* who the products are suitable for, for example holidays for 18–30-year-olds, meals for vegetarians.

Armed with this type of information, staff can advise customers what to buy or use based on what's available and the customer's needs. Customers also require information about the prices of products, opening times and the location of different facilities.

The more you know about the organisation you work for, the area in which you work and the travel and tourism industry in general, the more you will be able to help your customers. Imagine someone has spent fifteen hundred pounds on a holiday. He or she would expect to be given detailed information about the resort, the accommodation and the transfers.

Experience is something you can't replace and coupled with study and a thirst for more knowledge, staff can become experts in their particular field and so provide customers with all the information they need.

> **Think about it**
>
> Product knowledge is an essential part of the salesperson's armoury. If he/she doesn't know enough about the product or the benefits it offers it is highly unlikely that he/she will make the sale.
>
> What do you think you would need to know if a potential visitor rang up and asked you if it was worth visiting the theme park where you work?

The importance of customer service skills

Travel and tourism organisations rely on customers for their revenue, and travel and tourism staff rely on them for their jobs. That's why providing the right type of customer service is so important. That's why people working in travel and tourism should possess the necessary personal skills so that customers will buy their products, hopefully on a continuous basis.

Communicating with customers is a skill every employee working with customers should be taught. Possibly the most important aspect is understanding. Staff can talk to or write to customers as much as they like but if customers don't understand what is being stated there would be little point.

Using appropriate language

The way in which we say things is just as important as what we say. Travel and tourism employees who use language well will communicate clearly with their customers. Verbal communication, either face to face or on the phone, will have an effect on what customers think of staff and the organisation.

In customer service situations the language used should be simple and easy to understand. This is because communication is not just about sending a message; it is about receiving and understanding it.

There are some simple tips to remember when communicating with customers. First of all, any communication should not be complicated by using difficult language. Speaking clearly and concentrating on what is being said helps get the message across. This is especially true in using the phone when your voice should be made to sound interesting by altering its pitch and tone. This prevents the person at the other end losing interest. Listen to a travel consultant in action on the phone to see how it is done properly. Their enthusiasm is almost but not quite overwhelming.

Positive body language

Not all communication involves using words. Feelings, thoughts and attitudes can be conveyed without speaking by using gestures or facial expressions. This is known as non-verbal communication or body language.

Because sight is a more developed sense than hearing, body language is a very powerful form of face-to-face communication. In fact, 80 per cent of all communication is non-verbal. The ability to read someone's body language, especially when dealing with customers, allows travel and tourism staff to work out how their customers are feeling. This is a very powerful tool to possess. It becomes even more powerful when you are able to be aware of the messages your own body language is sending.

Positive body language includes making eye contact to show that you are listening to and are interested in the person who is talking to you. Open body language using welcoming gestures and smiles says to the customer you are not aggressive or hostile. Perhaps the most powerful and positive type of body language is a smile. This says two things: you like the customer and want to help them; you like your job and take pride in what you do.

Listening to customers

Travel and tourism employees have to listen carefully to customers at all times and ensure they understand what a customer is asking for.

Listening is the receiving role in spoken communication and is just as important as sending information accurately. Some reminders to ensure good listening skills include:

* Listen with an open mind; everyone's range of interests has its limits. We have a tendency to ignore ideas that are of no personal interest to us. This is a natural human trait.

* Be aware of your own prejudices; try to listen from a neutral position rather than let your own views colour your judgement. Guard against the tendency to resist or dismiss ideas if they do not coincide with your own views.

* Listen all the way through. Do not jump to conclusions. Remember the ratio of listening to talking should be 80:20.

* Learn to use thinking time wisely; try to identify the theme of the other person's message and check your understanding of facts by asking questions.

* Practise active listening skills; in some situations, particularly when there has already been a misunderstanding, it is important that the other person is reassured that you have fully understood their point of view.

Active listening is made up of
* mirroring . . . reflecting back the feelings
* paraphrasing . . . reflecting back the facts
* summarising . . . reflecting back the facts and feelings.

Listening can be hard work and requires concentration. However it is a skill that can be developed and it will help you gain valuable customer feedback, which can be used to improve the service even more.

Skills practice

This activity will test your listening skills. Working in pairs, one of you has to play the part of a customer, the other a travel consultant.
* The customer has to prepare a script lasting about two minutes describing the fantastic time he has just spent on holiday. It would actually bore most people to death but as a travel consultant you have to look interested. When the customer has finished you have to prove you have been paying attention by repeating the main details about the holiday.
* Reverse the roles but use a different situation, for example a day out at a theme park.

Dealing with customers over the phone

Customers use the phone when they want to communicate or find out information quickly. Many travel and tourism organisations, such as reservations centres, use the telephone as the main method of communication when dealing with customer enquiries.

Good telephone skills enable the standard of service customers expect to be met or even exceeded as good telephone techniques can create an excellent impression of the organisation.

A good telephone manner is an important communication skill for all travel and tourism employees who have to make or receive calls as part of their job.

Research by BT shows that on the telephone 14 per cent of our total communication is transmitted by the actual words used and 86 per cent by the way they are vocalised – i.e. how they sound.

The following techniques give an idea of how telephone communication should be carried out.

Taking a phone call

* Answer the call within three rings.
* Greet the caller with 'Good Morning' or 'Good Afternoon' and give the name of the organisation.
* Ask, 'How may I help you?'
* Sound bright and friendly by smiling – it makes a big difference to the sound of your voice.
* Keep paper and pencils next to the phone and make clear notes. To assure the caller that all details have been recorded accurately, read them back.
* Don't keep the caller holding on for a long time while you look for information or for the person they want to speak to.

* When transferring a call, give the caller any important information (such as the name of the person to whom you are transferring).

* Give your colleague important information (such as who it is on the line and what they need) before putting the call through.

* At the end of the call, check that the caller is satisfied with what you have said and done and are going to do.

* Use the caller's name when saying goodbye. Thank them for calling and let them put down the receiver first. This is not only polite, but also gives them a final chance to ask any more questions.

Making a phone call

The same techniques apply when making an outgoing call. Be clear about what you want to say and make notes of the key points you want to cover and have to hand any additional information such as the customer file or correspondence. This will also help if you need to leave a message on the answer phone.

Taking phone messages

If a message for a colleague or customer is not taken and delivered accurately, the impression of the organisation is likely to be poor. Try to follow a set procedure when taking messages and include:

* The name, title and telephone number of the caller

* The date and time of the call

* A clear and concise message

* The name of the person taking the message.

Make sure that everybody knows the system for messages reaching their destinations – are they delivered, do people have to collect them?

Dealing with answer phone messages

When a customer gets through to an answer phone or voicemail that too is creating an impression. The pre-recorded message should be clear and the instructions should be easy to follow. Also be sure to check all messages left on the answer phone as soon as possible, so that callers get a timely response. This applies equally to e-mail messages.

Think about it

What do you think the following expressions mean in relation to using the phone:
* 'Smile as you dial and dial a smile'
* 'Don't phone a groan'
Why should you sound enthusiastic on the phone? How can you sound enthusiastic on the phone?

Written communication

The way communication is presented in writing can affect customers' overall impression of the organisation. In other words, poor grammar, spelling mistakes and a format which is set out incorrectly, create a bad impression.

The importance of the written word is that is should mean exactly what it says. This refers again to all types of written communication including e-mails, letters, memos, faxes and notes.

CASE STUDY

Getting it 'write'

The following letter was sent out by a coach operator to a customer confirming a booking for a weekend trip to the Lake District. Identify the deliberate mistakes.

> 16 St Mary's Court
> New Street
> Oldham
>
> Hayward's Coaches
> High Street
> Blackburn
>
> 30/09/05
>
> Dear Sir,
>
> Thank you for your booking of last week for a 3 day trip to the lake district. The total cost is £250 and I look forward to recieving your payment in a weeks' time.
>
> The accommodation will be in a 4 star hotel and will cosist or breakfast and evening meal.
>
> Here's hoping you enjoy yourselves.
>
> Yours sincerely
>
> Peter Hayward
>
> Mannager
> Hayward's coaches.

In travel and tourism, written communication includes brochures, tickets, timetables, advertisements and information guides. In all these examples, written communication should be easy to understand and properly set out.

Written requests from customers not only need to be answered clearly but also speedily. This shows they are not being ignored, so an acknowledgement and response in writing, say within three days, will show the customer their request is being dealt with speedily. It also shows the organisation values the customer's correspondence.

Successful selling techniques

There have probably been more books written on 'How to Sell . . .' than any other subject, probably because without successful sales businesses will not survive, hence the demand for such books.

Selling is a technique. There is no such thing as a 'born salesman' (salesperson). Products can look attractive and be affordable but they won't sell themselves, they need someone to say why customers really need them.

In order to attract and keep customers, travel and tourism organisations need to sell their products and services. Everyone who works in the industry, not just the sales department, has a part to play in selling the product to the customer. That's why it's important that travel and tourism organisations train their staff not only in selling specific products like holidays but also in selling the organisation as a whole by being able to provide product information, maintain good relations, handle complaints and generally give quality customer service.

More specifically, every travel and tourism organisation has to be profitable and the sale of products keep organisations in business as income is generated, costs are covered and profits are made. There's an expression which goes, 'Selling ain't telling, it's asking'. Basically this means that you first have to find out what customers really want from a product, then, and only then, can you sell the benefits of the product.

Let us look at a sales situation step by step.

Step 1 Creating a good first impression In general people will only buy a product if they can like and trust the person who is doing the selling. If customers are suspicious that they are being 'sold to', dislike the salesperson or feel tense in any way, they become sales resistant. It is therefore essential that the first impression customers receive is one of warmth, trust and friendliness. This puts the customers at ease and helps the salesperson establish a rapport with them.

Step 2 Find out what the customer wants This can only happen by listening to them and asking questions. For example, a customer in a travel agency might want a holiday in Spain. In order to establish exactly what they want the travel consultant can ask:

* When would you like to go?

* What type of area do you want to visit?

* What price range are you looking at?

* How long do you want to go for?

* How many people will be going?

* What sort of hotel would you like to stay in?

* What do you want out of your holiday?

Do not think you are being nosy by asking all these questions. The customer will realise that you are taking a great interest in them and will be only too happy to answer your questions.

Step 3 Sampling the products Once you have established what the customer wants, you can then give them a sample of products they may be interested in. Again, listen to what they say, look at their body language and answer any questions they may have.

Now is a good time to sell the benefits of the products, in other words what advantages there will be to the customer if they buy your products. For example,

'You can fly from Nottingham East Midlands Airport, which means you only have half an hour drive from home.'

or

'The hotel is less than half a mile from the beach so you will only have a five-minute walk before you get down to some serious sunbathing.'

or

'If you travel just before the high season you will save up to £200 per person.'

These are all attractive benefits which any customer will have difficulty resisting.

Step 4 Closing the sale This is a part of the sale that many people shy away from. It is easy to lose everything at this stage. No sale is made until it is closed, and that is when the customer decides to buy. The open questions you have asked previously can now be changed to closed questions that require a 'yes' or 'no' answer.

This is also a time for reiterating the information the customer has given, allowing him or her to add extra information if you have missed anything, and then justify your choice of product by relating it back to the needs the customer has mentioned and confirmed to you.

If people were unwilling to enter into a financial exchange for the product you are offering, they would have stopped the conversation before this stage.

Selling and self-confidence

Selling doesn't come easy. Employees need to be trained in the art of selling. This can include role-play situations and watching salespeople in action. Practising sales skills helps build subject knowledge and leads to an increase in self-confidence.

Making that first sale is almost like an obstacle to overcome, and the feeling an employee gains from making a sale gives them satisfaction and motivation to sell even more. Motivation is even more apparent if sales are linked to commission, that is the more you sell, the more you earn.

Salespeople are made not born. Thorough training along with personality, a positive attitude and good subject knowledge will give the salesperson every chance of making the sale. They will need to have the confidence to show the customer the benefits of buying the product and the value it will have for them.

Telesales

Many sales are made other than through face-to-face meetings. Telephone selling has grown hugely in recent years and demands special techniques of selling.

It may begin with a potential customer phoning a travel agent to ask about holidays. Obviously the customer wants to go on holiday and there are clear 'buying signals' if they start asking about prices, dates and accommodation. Faced with such situations the travel agent needs to have the required product knowledge to answer the customer's questions confidently, quickly and satisfactorily.

Telephone selling of products and services is also initiated by companies. They will phone an existing customer or a potential new customer with details and special offers on products or services without knowing whether the person they are calling is interested in buying these. This is called 'cold selling'. It is a practice used to sell various kinds of products and services, for example double glazing, motor insurance and financial products. Many travel and tourism products are also sold in this way, using a database of information about consumers to target prospective customers.

Though many people are offended by this selling techique and refuse to purchase in this way, there are many who find it convenient and are willing to purchase, for example, last-minute low-price holiday deals over the phone.

The Internet

The Internet has had a huge impact on the purchasing behaviour of consumers in recent times. New companies have been formed and existing ones have developed their marketing to take advantage of the potential of the Internet for selling products and services to consumers.

The travel and tourism industry has recognised the trend towards buying holidays or making travel arrangements through the Internet. The products of the industry are now extensively advertised through company websites, giving consumers easy access to information and choosing the arrangements that suit them: flights, accommodation, insurance and car hire can all be organised in this way.

Even travel agents, who experienced a downturn in business because of the effect of the Internet, have set up their own websites to compete with those organisations that sell their products solely through the Internet. However, the Internet still exerts considerable pressure on the business of travel agents.

Think about it

There will be times when a customer decides not to buy. You have to try and accept this with good grace. There's nothing wrong by saying to the customer, 'If you have a change of mind you know where to contact us.'

Many salespeople hate it when a customer says 'I will think about it'. Why is this?

Tact and diplomacy

There are occasions when a customer thinks he or she is right when in fact they are not. Take for example a customer who returns from holiday and complains to the travel agent that the location of the hotel, the entertainment offered and the types of excursions they could go on were not as described in the brochure. It turns out that the hotel they had looked at was not their hotel but one in a nearby resort! How do you handle that? The following action could be taken:

∗ Most importantly, listen to all the facts and do not interrupt – this gives you time to come up with a suitable response

∗ Remain calm and don't argue

∗ Check the brochure details and point out that the description applied to another hotel but you can see why they thought it was applicable to their hotel because it was on the same page

∗ Empathise with the customer and say that you understand how the misunderstanding arose

∗ Say you will communicate how the misunderstanding occurred to the marketing department in charge of the brochure production

∗ Once again, apologise that they were disappointed with their holiday.

Sometimes in situations like this customers will see the funny side of the misunderstanding or happily accept your explanation of how it came about. That will at least overcome any resentment However they may be reluctant to book another holiday with you out of embarrassment or they may well return saying 'Remember us?'

Remaining calm

No matter how good your service, you will never please everybody all the time. However, you will be more prepared to deal with any situation that arises if you are confident of your customer service skills, aware of the sort of things likely to cause problems and know the correct procedure to use in difficult situations.

The use of active listening techniques without arguing with a customer who is complaining will help the situation, especially if you can reassure the customer you have understood.

Try to remain calm and in control. If one person is calm and the other angry and out of control, onlookers are likely to think that the calm person is right, even if this is not the case.

If you don't have the authority or knowledge to deal effectively with a situation, refer it on to someone who does. Always make sure the customer knows what is going on and that colleagues are aware that dealing with this customer could be sensitive.

In some travel and tourism organisations, the responsibility for solving problems rests with managers and supervisors. However, it is useful to remember that 'a customer with a problem is everybody's problem'.

Dealing with different types of customers

Awkward customers

Some people are naturally awkward. There is no particular reason for being so, it's just part of their character. However awkward they are, they still have to be treated properly and if it means remaining ever cooler and calmer than normal, so be it.

Such people tend to complain more readily than other customers and know their rights. They are also aware that many organisations will offer some type of compensation if a customer complains.

Some of them will visit different places such as supermarkets, electrical goods stores, restaurants, pubs and travel agents, usually in search of compensation or to avoid paying the full price of a product by making a complaint about it. Eventually they become well known to these organisations who will tend to refuse them future service.

Travel and tourism organisations usually have procedures for dealing with customers who are unreasonable and abusive. Fortunately this type of customer is in the minority.

The procedures include staying calm and controlled and calling for support from a senior member of staff, if required. Some customers become angry, not necesarily because they are displeased with the product or even with the way they have been treated, but because of some problem in their personal life. So, you must listen and observe very closely to what they are saying and doing and act accordingly. However, never accept verbal abuse! If this occurs, call for support from your colleagues, or if it is serious enough, call the police.

Employees in the travel and tourism industry are trained to handle difficult situations. This is done through lectures on the issues and in role-play activities. The training has to be as realistic as possible in order for the employees to acquire the knowledge and confidence required for actually dealing with awkward customers.

People with special needs and disabilities

Anyone who works in customer service needs to understand the needs of customers with disabilities – whether mobility, sensory or learning impairment. It is particularly important to know about the specialist equipment and facilities available to customers. Many organisations, such as high street shops and hotels, deal with people with disabilities by providing lifts, ramps and wider car spaces near entrances to buildings.

Technical skills in travel and tourism

The travel and tourism industry has moved with the times when it comes to handling new technology. Employees are trained to operate Viewdata and reservations systems as well as process payments and exchange currency. These skills are learned through both internal and external training. This results in professional employees who are competent at using a wide range of skills necessary for working in the travel and tourism industry in the twenty-first century.

Knowledge check

1 What do we mean when we say organisations try to go the 'extra mile' to achieve customer satisfaction?

2 What do you think the term 'you only get one chance to make a good first impression' means?

3 What are the two most likely outcomes for a travel agent if clients leave feeling they have received 'value for money'?

4 How do you think customers feel about travel and tourism organisations that deal with complaints in a positive way?

5 Why is it important to make the induction process as interesting and motivating as possible for a new employee?

6 Why is training and development important to both the organisation and to the employee?

7 What does the following expression mean, 'Selling ain't telling, it's asking'?

8 How can travel and tourism organisations create a good public image?

9 What promotes good teamwork amongst staff?

10 How could you motivate employees who are not satisfied with their jobs?

11 Why is it important for employees in the travel and tourism industry to have in-depth product knowledge?

12 Why is it important nowadays to have the appropriate technical skills to work in the travel and tourism industry?

13 All customers have different needs. How different are the needs of the following people: individuals, groups, people with disabilities, senior citizens?

14 What is the best way of dealing with a very angry customer?

15 All customers think they are right, even when they are not! How would you deal with this type of customer?

UNIT ASSESSMENT

For this unit you have to produce a portfolio based on an investigation into aspects of customer service in a chosen travel and tourism organisation. You need to be aware of the importance of choosing an appropriate organisation to work with because input from the organisation and the collection of appropriate literature and resources is essential. So it may be an idea to choose an organisation with which you are familiar.

This unit makes up one-third of the total AS marks Single Award. It is assessed by your centre and moderated externally.

Your portfolio should include a review of induction procedures and training by your chosen organisation; a record of customer service role plays, demonstrating how you would meet the needs of different types of customer in your chosen organisation; an investigation into the product knowledge required by the organisation's employees; an evaluation of the range of skills required to deliver customer service.

You will be required to demonstrate your knowledge, understanding and skills of customer service and be able to apply such skills. You will have to use appropriate research techniques to obtain and analyse information, and finally you will have to evaluate that information in order to make judgements, draw conclusions and make recommendations.

Scenario

You are a management consultant who advises travel and tourism organisations on customer service. Your chosen organisation has invited you to advise them on how to improve their customer service as their sales have slumped recently and they have put this down to the level of service their clients have been receiving. Your job is to reverse this trend by reviewing the organisation's induction procedures, show staff how to meet the needs of different customers, investigate the amount of product knowledge the staff possess and the skills required in dealing with customers.

Task 1

Produce a thorough and detailed review of the appropriateness of the organisation's induction and training procedures, indicating how they benefit customers and the organisation. (up to 15 marks)

Task 2

Demonstrate in role-play situations a wide range of skills relating to the needs of different customer groups, showing sound product knowledge. You must try and respond in a positive way, successfully meeting the needs of different customer types. (up to 18 marks)

Task 3

Use your research skills independently to analyse how induction and training procedures provide employees with the product knowledge to enable them to provide first-class customer service. (up to 18 marks)

Task 4

Evaluate the full range of skills required to deliver customer service within the organisation and make sure all evidence is evaluated for appropriateness. You have to ensure your evaluation is well-structured and provides a full and detailed conclusion. (up to 9 marks)

UNIT 3

Travel destinations

Introduction

This unit is about the main travel destinations in Europe and North America visited by UK tourists and why people visit them. By the end of the unit you will be able to locate where the popular destinations are and identify the main transport routes and travel times to these places.

Different destinations appeal to different types of tourists. You will be able to consider the advantages and disadvantages of a variety of travel options for different types of tourists.

How you will be assessed

You will be assessed on your research skills by producing a portfolio of travel information for different types of customers travelling from the UK to two contrasting destinations, one in Europe and one in North America. Your portfolio will contain information on where these destinations are located and a description of their key geographical characteristics and main attractions.

You will be asked to produce a script for a welcome meeting at each destination linking suitable tourist facilities to different customers. You will need to advise on the best method of travel to each destination and produce maps to inform your clients.

To complete the assessment you will need to provide research evidence to evaluate the appeal of each destination to different groups of tourists and evaluate their future popularity as a travel destination.

After studying this unit you should have learned about:

* The range of tourist destinations
* Research skills
* Tourist generating and receiving areas
* Tourist appeal
* Different types of transport.

The range of tourist destinations

A *travel destination* is the end point of a journey. People travel to a destination for a variety of different reasons, including holiday, business or visiting friends and relatives. A *tourist destination* combines travel with facilities and attractions that appeal to tourists. People working in the travel and tourism industry need to know where the major tourist destinations are and be able to describe the main features of these destinations.

People working in the travel and tourism industry need to be able to identify:

* The location of continents and oceans
* The location of major tourist destinations
* The location of major cities
* The climate of major destinations
* The natural and built attractions of major destinations
* The tourist facilities at the destinations
* Travel times to different destinations
* The main travel routes and gateways to major destinations.

This knowledge is important when advising clients about their travel plans, for example when working in a travel agency. You may be required to develop new tourism products seeking out potential tourist destinations for a tour operator. You may also be working with other travel and tourism organisations in different places around the world so a familiarity with tourism geography will help you gain an understanding of different places.

Key terms

Travel destination The end point of a journey.
Tourist destination A place with facilities and attractions that attract tourists.

The location of continents and oceans

A *continent* is a large continuous area of land on the surface of the Earth. There are seven continents:

* Africa
* Asia
* Australia
* North America
* South America
* Europe
* Antarctica.

An *ocean* is a large area of salt water on the surface of the Earth. Oceans cover 71 per cent of the Earth's surface. The five major oceans are:

* Antarctic (or Southern)
* Arctic
* Atlantic
* Indian
* Pacific.

Skills practice

Using an atlas identify each of the continents and the oceans.

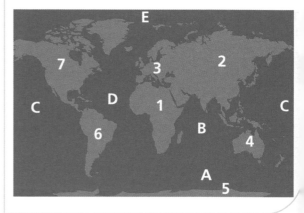

The location of major tourist destinations

Major tourist destinations have developed because they have good transport networks and are able to cater for the needs of large numbers of tourists. A destination that is a relatively short flight of less than five hours from the UK is known as a *short-haul* destination. The major short-haul tourist destinations are found within Europe, the most popular being Spain and France. *Long haul* describes flights of more than five hours, which tend to be beyond Europe, the most popular destinations being the USA and Canada.

Europe is defined by the countries in geographical Europe, within which some countries have joined the European Union.

Skills practice

1 Using an atlas and a blank map of Europe (on page 142) identify each of the countries represented by geographical Europe.

2 Using the information in Table 3.1, add the information to your map of Europe. You may wish to use a colour code key.

3 Suggest reasons why Spain and France are popular travel destinations with tourists from the UK.

Table 3.1 The top 10 short-haul destinations from the UK in 2004

Rank order	Country	Number of visits abroad by UK residents (000s)
1	Spain	13,807
2	France	11,602
3	Irish Republic	4112
4	Italy	2968
5	Greece	2701
6	Germany	2332
7	Netherlands	2161
8	Belgium	1799
9	Portugal	1797
10	Cyprus	1280

In comparison the USA receives 4,173,000 visits and Canada receives 615,000 visits as long-haul destinations from the UK.

Source: Office for National Statistics (2005)

Within the countries in Table 3.1 certain destinations become popular with tourists and develop attractions and facilities that makes them into major tourist resorts. These places continue to attract large numbers of UK tourists.

The choice of destination can depend on the season. Both summer sun and winter sun holiday brochures suggest an escape to warmer climates, however some destinations are more popular at different times of the year. The most popular travel destinations for UK tourists buying package holidays with TUI are:

Summer	Winter
1 Majorca	1 Tenerife
2 Ibiza	2 Costa Blanca
3 Costa Blanca	3 Gran Canaria
4 Costa del Sol	4 Lanzarote
5 Tenerife	5 Costa del Sol
6 Minorca	6 Majorca
7 Corfu	7 Paphos, Cyprus
8 Paphos, Cyprus	8 Fuerteventura
9 Gran Canaria	9 Tunisia
10 Lanzarote	10 Sharm El Sheikh

Source: TUI (2004)

Skills practice

1 Label the top 10 summer and winter travel destinations on the blank map of Europe (on page 142), using a suitable key.

2 Identify which destinations are long haul and which are short haul.

3 Which destinations appear as both summer and winter resorts? Suggest why they are popular all year round.

4 Would the list of popular travel destinations be different for another tour operator? Give reasons for your answer.

Major travel destinations that are popular with UK tourists include:

The Algarve, Portugal

The Algarve is located on the southern coast of Portugal and is surrounded on both sides by the

Figure 3.1 The Algarve

Atlantic Ocean. It has an attractive coastline with nearly one hundred sandy beaches. The resorts are relatively low key (few night clubs but many quiet local bars and restaurants) and the area has many world-class golf courses. The long summers are hot and dry. The region receives the most international visitors to Portugal and the majority are from the UK.

The Spanish Costas, Spain

Figure 3.2 The Spanish Costas

The Spanish Costas are found along the southern coastline, on the shore of the Mediterranean Sea.

These areas are some of the most popular tourist destinations in Europe and are known for their sandy beaches and their high-rise hotels. By moving along the coastline away from the Costas quieter beaches can be found along with more historical and cultural attractions.

Costa del Sol stretches from Almeria to Tarifa. The main resort of Torremolinos has a reputation for being overcrowded due to its rapid development and its popularity with tourists.

Costa Brava lies northeast of Barcelona. Some of the resorts, such as Tossa de Mar, remain largely undeveloped, despite attracting large numbers of visitors, compared to resorts such as Loret de Mar.

Costa Blanca has also seen much recent development with the towns of Benidorm and Alicante becoming major tourist resorts. Temperatures are warmer than on the Costa Brava and the beaches are wider. The Terra Mitica Theme Park, Benidorm, offers an alternative to those who wish to venture away from the beaches.

Florida, USA

Figure 3.3 Florida

Florida is famous for its built attractions of Disney World, Universal Studios, Sea World and Busch Gardens in Orlando. To the south, Florida Keys offers many beaches and clear blue waters that are popular with divers. The city of Miami offers the chance for a city break and a visit to Miami Beach that is often frequented by celebrities.

The Grand Canyon, USA

Figure 3.4 The Grand Canyon

The Grand Canyon is found in the Grand Canyon National Park in the state of Arizona and has been described as one of the 'must see' natural attractions in the world. The valley is visited by 5 million people each year and is over 1.61 kilometres (1 mile deep) and between 6.44 to 18.96 kilometres across (4 to 18 miles).

Think about it

In groups consider why these holiday destinations are popular with UK tourists.

Skills practice

1 Using a range of travel brochures identify five travel destinations in Europe and five travel destinations in the USA and Canada that are popular with UK tourists. Locate each destination on a map.

2 Identify the main attractions of each travel destination and suggest the types of tourist who would be interested in visiting them.

The location of major cities

Major cities provide a destination for city breaks, which is the fastest growing sector of international travel. It is not just the capital cities that benefit, other large cities offer services for conference visitors. Most people who go on city breaks tend to be from the middle- to high-income groups and therefore city breaks are less affected by economic decline. Europeans tend to take two or more city breaks a year in addition to their main annual holiday. Low-cost airlines have expanded the choice of destinations even further.

The most popular cities visited by UK tourists are:

1	Paris	6	Brussels
2	Amsterdam	7	Bruges
3	Dublin	8	Barcelona
4	Rome	9	Venice
5	Prague	10	Vienna.

Source: ABTA (2004)

Skills practice

1 Locate each of the ten most popular cities in Europe visited by UK tourists on the blank map of Europe (see page 142).

2 For each of the most popular cities visited by UK tourists, identify one major visitor attraction in each city.

3 Using a range of travel brochures identify ten cities in the USA and Canada that are visited by UK tourists. Plot these on the blank outline map (see page 143).

The climate of major destinations and why this affects their appeal

Think about it

Why is climate important in attracting visitors from the UK?

Climate affects the appeal of destinations. It is the second most important reason for choosing a holiday destination, after the price of the holiday. Climate is important because warmer climates are more often attractive to tourists from the UK.

Climate is a measure of atmospheric conditions such as temperature, sunshine and rainfall that are based on yearly or monthly averages over a period of not less than thirty years. These figures are usually displayed in holiday brochures, holiday guides and atlases.

Weather conditions are events that occur daily and form part of the climate for the destination. People prefer warm, bright sunny conditions rather than cold, damp and overcast ones. Comfort is very important; whether a person is sunbathing or skiing, they must feel comfortable otherwise they will not enjoy their holiday.

Major destinations tend to be in warmer climates. Colder climates also have an appeal but receive smaller numbers of visitors. One exception to this rule is the popular ski resorts that rely on an abundance of snow.

Precipitation

Precipitation is the measure of rainfall, snow or hail. Climate data can show the average amount of precipitation per month and is usually displayed in millimetres (mm). This gives the visitor an idea whether they are visiting during a wet or dry season.

Temperature

Temperature can be measured in degrees Centigrade (°C) or degrees Fahrenheit (°F). In Europe most of the travel brochures display temperatures in Centigrade, in America most of the travel brochures display temperatures in Fahrenheit. Although 75°F sounds a lot more than 24°C, in fact they are the same temperature. Travel brochures often display average monthly temperatures or average minimum and maximum monthly temperatures.

Humidity

Humidity describes the amount of water vapour that is present in the atmosphere and is measured as a percentage. The warmer the atmosphere is, potentially the more water the atmosphere can hold. High humidity over 70 per cent can make visitors feel sticky and uncomfortable. Where areas of high humidity and high temperatures exist, these are potentially unsuitable for tourist development.

Hours of sunshine

Hours of sunshine depends on the amount of cloud. The more cloud there is the less sunshine there is.

The UK receives on average 53 days of sunshine each year; this is one reason why so many Britons travel overseas to search for more sun.

The affects on climate

Destinations that have a similar climate can experience differences in sunshine, temperature, rainfall and humidity. These differences are due to geographical features, including the proximity of the sea, being inland, height of land and wind direction.

Destinations that are close to the sea tend to be cooler in the summer and warmer in the winter, whereas destinations in the middle of continents or inland, tend to have warmer summers and colder winters.

The height of the land affects climate. The higher the land the colder it is. For example, in the Alps the temperature drops by 0.75°C for every 100 metres ascent on north-facing slopes. Higher altitudes also mean more precipitation. This is particularly important in alpine regions where winter sports destinations rely on a generous amount of snow. In Southern Europe mountain regions have allowed the development of some winter sports, including the Sierra Nevada in Spain. Winter sports are also popular in the USA; Aspen, Colorado, in particular is famous for its skiing.

Adventure holidays and package tours have extended the choice of locations into the fringes of hot desert areas and cold regions. These give tourists a different experience and are usually made available during the most favourable times of the year due to the extreme climatic conditions.

Air pollution can also affect the amount of sunshine. In Los Angeles the amount of smog caused by air pollution reduces the amount of sunlight.

Key terms

Climate The average temperature, sunshine and rainfall of an area or place over a period of time.

Weather The climatic events on a particular day at a particular area or place.

CASE STUDY

Hurricanes in Florida

An important affect on the appeal of major destinations is the threat of hazardous climatic conditions. The Caribbean Islands and the state of Florida, USA, both suffer from hurricanes and tropical storms. The official hurricane season lasts from 1 June to 30 November with early to mid-September receiving most of the storms. Hurricanes tend not to affect the tourism industry but in September 2004 four hurricanes hit the American state of Florida, the first time that this has happened since records began in 1851. Wind speeds were recorded between 75 and 140 mph. Over 2.5 million residents were evacuated.

Tourism is Florida's largest industry and is worth $50 billion a year. It is America's second-most popular holiday destination after California. The hurricanes caused the major tourist attractions including Sea World, Universal Studios and Disney World to temporarily close. Hotel bookings began to decline as hotels in Miami and Tampa received 22 per cent fewer bookings than the same time the previous year.

During the hurricanes most UK tour operators allowed visitors booked to travel to Florida to make changes to their travel plans free of charge, as many had decided to change their choice of destination.

CASE STUDY

Tourism threatened by climate change

Heat waves, droughts, rising seas, flash floods, forest fires and diseases could turn profitable tourist destinations into holiday horror stories according to new research published by the World Wildlife Fund. Tour operators and countries relying on tourism will need to take into account the potential impacts of climate change when planning new resorts or upgrading their facilities.

Dr David Viner, Senior Research Scientist at the University of East Anglia, who compiled the study, warned: 'Areas such as the Mediterranean, a popular destination for British tourists, could become unbearable during the traditional summer holiday season. As temperatures begin to soar, many tourists will stay away.'

Source: World Wildlife Fund UK (1999)

Skills practice

1 Using the above two case studies explain how climate has an important impact on the appeal of travel destinations.

2 What are the problems associated with extreme weather and climate in tourist areas?

3 What can be done to help reduce the effect of extreme changes in climate? Explain how your recommendations will have an impact on the tourism industry.

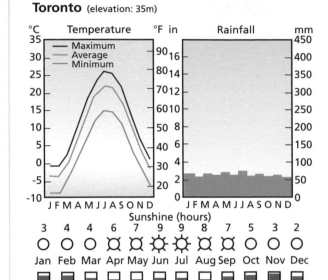

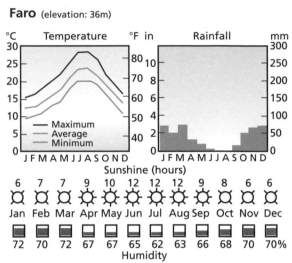

Figure 3.5 Climate graphs for Toronto and Faro

1 Using an atlas locate the two destinations above on a map.

2 For each destination identify the hottest month and the coldest month of the year in °C.

3 For each destination compare the annual temperature range (hottest to coldest monthly average) in °C.

4 For each destination what is the annual average temperature?

5 For each destination identify the wettest and the driest months.

6 For each destination identify the month that receives the most sunshine.

7 Which is the most popular holiday destination? Give reasons for your answer.

The natural and built attractions of major destinations

Major destinations can either provide natural or built attractions or both.

Natural attractions

Natural attractions are based on the *topography* or shape of the land. Each destination has its own unique topography, which can be attractive to tourists.

Natural attractions can include:

* Lakes
* Rivers
* Caves
* Volcanoes
* Forests
* Mountains
* Coastlines
* Waterfalls.

> **Think about it**
>
> Discuss a natural attraction that you have visited and give reasons as to why you found it interesting.

Lakes

Lakes are large inland areas of water. They provide an attraction to tourists, including those seeking scenic beauty and water sports.

CASE STUDY

The Italian Lakes

The Italian Lakes is a popular destination for UK tourists. Based in the region of Trentino in the north of Italy, the lakes are surrounded by the Dolomite Mountain range to the north. The lakes are deep and have steep sides producing a dramatic landscape.

There are four main lakes:

- Lake Como
- Lake Garda
- Lake Lugano
- Lake Maggiore.

Lake Garda is the largest lake in Italy and is the most developed in terms of tourism with many small towns and camping sites situated along the shore. A mild climate and rich fertile soils have encouraged olives, lemon trees and grape vines to flourish. The steep sides of Lake Garda can reach up to 1750 metres (5775 feet) at Monte Baldo. Views across the Lake are possible from a panoramic rotating cable car.

The Trentino Tourist Board has encouraged the growth of tourism based on natural attractions. These include:

- Wine tourism
- Dairy and local food tourism
- Mountain bike holidays
- Horse riding holidays through the mountains
- Windsurfing holidays.

nuova funivia panoramica
neue Panorama - Seilbahn
new panoramic cableway

MALCESINE - MONTE BALDO

MALCESINE - MONTE BALDO
Lago di Garda m. 100 - 1750 Gardasee

Skills practice

Complete the following table for one lakeland region in Europe and one in North America:

	One lakeland region in Europe	One lakeland region in North America
Location		
Appeal of the main attractions		
Description of climate		

Rivers

Lakes and oceans are fed by a series of *rivers*. Rivers can be a popular destination for their scenic beauty, wildlife and fishing. Over sixty per cent of UK river cruise passengers travel to European destinations. The large European rivers of the Rhine and the Danube are linked by the Main River and a series of canals. This allows cruises to take place from the North Sea to the Black Sea along 3500 kilometres (2200 miles) of waterway. Popular cruises include trips from Frankfurt to Munich and from Amsterdam to Vienna and Budapest.

Cruises on the River Rhine allow passengers to explore towns and cities and the many castles that can be seen from the river.

The top five European destinations for UK river cruise passengers in 2002 were:

1   River Rhine and Moselle
2   River Danube
3   River Rhone and Seine
4   The Russian waterways
5   River Po.

Source: Mintel (2004)

Forests

Forests provide unique habitats for wildlife and are popular destinations for walking and activity holidays. The Black Forest in southern Germany is famous for its highland scenery, cuckoo clocks, fairy-tale castles and the cherry schnapps that is used to make the famous Black Forest Gateau. The forest is over 200 kilometres (125 miles) long and 60 kilometres (37 miles) wide, with mountain peaks of up to 1500 metres (5000 feet). The Black Forest runs along a stretch of the River Rhine and also borders other tourist regions that are famous for their natural attractions; these include Lake Constance in Switzerland and the Alsace region of France.

Mountains

Mountains form dramatic landscapes that often have snow on the highest peaks. This is in contrast to the deep valleys that often contain lakes and rivers. The Rocky Mountains extend from Alaska, through Canada and the USA, to Mexico. The valley beneath the Canadian Rockies contains Highway 93, which allows visitors to explore the National Parks of Banff and Jasper. These tourist destinations have been popular for over one hundred years and combine summer hiking with winter skiing.

Skills practice

Using the blank outline maps of Europe and North America (pages 142 and 143) and an atlas, identify the mountainous areas and using a key mark on your map ten popular mountainous tourist destinations, five in Europe and five in North America.

Mountains provide dramatic landscapes for tourists to explore

Forests provide opportunities for activity holidays

Caves

A *cave* is a natural hole in a rock, occurring most commonly in areas of limestone, although caves can occur in any type of rock. Caves can be spectacular and have columns of stalagmites that rise from the floor and stalactites that hang from the ceiling.

CASE STUDY

Show caves at Nerja, Spain

The show caves at Nerja, on the Costa del Sol in Spain, are situated 3 kilometres (1.9 miles) from the coast on the slopes of the Sierra Almijara mountains. The caves are 4823 metres (15,916 feet) long and over five million years old, and have been carved out by the gradual erosion of water. They have the widest column of rock in the world, the grand centre column found in the *Sala del Cataclismo* (Cataclysm Hall), which is 32 metres (105 feet) high, and 13 × 7 metres (43 × 23 feet) wide. Ancient wall paintings can also be seen in the caves as they were inhabited from 25,000 BC until the Bronze Age. The centre of the caves has been transformed into a performance area where music concerts and ballets are accompanied by a light show that illuminates the large columns of rock.

Show caves at Nerja

Skills practice

Describe another cave that attracts tourists from the UK, in either Europe or North America. Suggest why people visit this natural attraction.

Volcanoes

A *volcano* is an opening of the Earth's surface where magma, molten rock or ash erupts, often violently. Most volcanoes tend to be conical in shape and are found where there is a weakness in the Earth's crust. Volcanoes are popular with tourists who enjoy watching the spectacle from a safe distance, but when volcanoes are active they are dangerous.

Mount St Helens in Washington USA, stands at 2549 metres high (8411 feet) and erupted on 18 May 1980 with devastating effect. Over 400 metres of the volcano was blown away and the eruption cloud stood at 19 kilometres (12 miles) high. During the eruption 57 people lost their lives and the damage caused by the volcano cost over $1 billion. Further eruptions were recorded in 2004 with accompanying earthquakes. Mount St Helens is becoming more active and potentially could erupt again at any time in the near future.

Think about it

Discuss the impact that Mount St Helens has on tourism to the local area.

Skills practice

Complete the details for Mount Etna and Mount Vesuvius in following table:

	Mount Etna, Italy	Mount Vesuvius, Italy
Location		
Date of last eruption		
Description of the eruption		
Why tourists visit the volcano		

Coastlines

Coastlines are the most popular natural attractions. They can be dramatic with steep cliffs and crashing waves. These areas are exposed to powerful waves that erode the coastline. Other parts can be relaxing with sandy or pebble beaches. The coastline can offer many leisure opportunities, from sitting in the sun to taking part in water sports, beach sports or children's entertainment.

The coastlines in Europe are awarded a Blue Flag when the beach and water quality meets the standard of the European Union Bathing Water Directive. The eco-label is administered by the Foundation for Environmental Education in Europe (FEEE) and beaches are assessed on an annual basis. If a beach does not match the required standards the award can be taken away. The award has been given to nearly 3000 beaches and marinas in 24 countries across Europe and has been extended to South Africa.

The top ten countries in Europe with the largest areas of coastline are:

1	Norway	6	Turkey
2	Greece	7	Croatia
3	UK	8	Iceland
4	Italy	9	Spain
5	Denmark	10	Estonia.

Canada has the largest coastal area in the world with 202,080 kilometres (125,492 miles) and the United States has 19,924 kilometres (12,373 miles) of coastline.

Think about it

Discuss the reasons why some areas of coastline are developed for tourism whilst others are left in a relatively natural state.

Skills practice

1 For each of the top ten countries in Europe with the largest areas of coastline identify one major coastal resort and list the main attractions that exist.

2 Using a range of travel brochures identify five popular coastal resorts in Canada and five in the United States. List their main attractions and identify the type of visitor they would appeal to.

Skills practice

1 Is it important that a beach resort receives a Blue Flag? Give reasons for your answer.

2 Does a similar beach eco-label scheme exist in North America? Give examples of areas of coastline that are considered to be of high environmental quality.

Waterfalls

Waterfalls can be an impressive sight and are popular with visitors. Niagara Falls is the second largest waterfall in the world after Victoria Falls in southern Africa. Niagara Falls is located between Lake Erie and Lake Ontario on the border between Canada and the United States and is comprised of three waterfalls: the American Falls, the Bridal Veil Falls and the Canadian/Horseshoe Falls. The height of the waterfalls stands at approximately 52 metres (170 feet) with the water flowing at speeds between 150,000 and 600,000 US gallons per second. At the bottom of the Niagara Falls the water travels for 9.3 kilometres (15 miles) along deep and narrow valleys, known as gorges, until entering Lake Ontario. Niagara Falls attracts over 12 million tourists each year. At night the waterfalls are illuminated by powerful coloured spotlights, providing a colourful spectacle.

Think about it

Why do you think people find waterfalls so appealing?

Niagara Falls

Built attractions

Built attractions include a wide variety of purpose-built venues. Some have been adapted to meet the needs of tourists.

Built attractions include:

* Theme parks

* Indoor arenas

* Historic buildings

* Ancient monuments

* Museums and art galleries.

Theme parks

Theme parks are purpose-built visitor attractions offering a wide range of facilities including shopping, restaurants and gardens. The parks are themed around historic events, fantasy, childhood or a futuristic world. Many contain 'white knuckle rides' but increasingly they have become more sophisticated in terms of their use of fantasy and illusion.

Theme parks offer value for money in that they provide a full day's entertainment at a fixed price. Pricing structures often allow discounts for groups and for families. Details of special offers are usually displayed on a theme park's website. Even when the weather conditions are poor many theme parks contain attractions which people can enjoy in the wet as well as having a range of indoor attractions

and facilities. Some theme parks are specifically targeted at families and younger children, whereas others have more exhilarating rides attracting teenagers and young adults. Although most visitors to theme parks are day visitors, many theme parks are encouraging visitors to stay overnight in purpose-built themed accommodation.

Skills practice

Complete the following table with the details and main features of popular theme parks in Europe:

THEME PARK	LOCATION	MAIN FEATURES
Disneyland	Paris	
Efteling		
Europa Park		
Futuroscope		
Gardaland		
Legoland		
Parc Asterix		
Phantasialand		
Port Aventura		
Tivoli Gardens		

Purpose-built attractions such as theme parks provide a wide range of facilities for visitors

CASE STUDY

Popular theme parks

The Magic Kingdom at Florida's Disney World is the number-one most visited theme park in the world, with 14 million visitors per year. It is not just a theme park but a purpose-built resort in its own right, including hotels, shops, entertainment, live music venues, a sports complex and six golf courses. The emphasis is on family fun and the attractions have been designed with this in mind. For younger visitors It's a Small World and The Magic Adventures of Winnie the Pooh contrast with Splash Mountain and Space Mountain for the older and more adventurous visitors. The Magic Kingdom covers 122 square kilometres (47 square miles), however not all the land has been developed as 25 per cent of the resort has been designated as a wilderness preserve. The Magic Kingdom is the largest employer in Florida, employing 50,000 people. More than 46 million colas are consumed each year at Disney World Resort along with 7 million hamburgers and 5 million hot dogs.

The top ten most visited theme parks in North America (2003) are:

1 The Magic Kingdom at Disney World, Lake Buena Vista, Florida (14 million visitors)

2 Disneyland, Anaheim, California (12.7 million visitors)

3 Epcot at Disney World, Lake Buena Vista, Florida (8.6 million)

4 Disney-MGM Studios at Disney World, Lake Buena Vista, Florida (7.8 million visitors)

5 Disney's Animal Kingdom at Disney World, Lake Buena Vista, Florida (7.3 million visitors)

6 Universal Studios at Universal Orlando (6.8 million visitors)

7 Islands of Adventure at Universal Orlando (6 million visitors)

8 Disney's California Adventures, Anaheim, California (5.3 million visitors)

9 SeaWorld Florida, Orlando, Florida (5.2 million visitors)

10 Universal Studios Hollywood, Universal City, California (4.5 million visitors).

Source: Amusement Business (2004)

Think about it

Why do the top ten theme parks in the United States attract so many visitors?

Indoor arenas

Indoor arenas provide a variety of public exhibitions, entertainment, music events and sporting facilities, as well as business exhibitions (trade shows) and conventions. They are large enough to support exhibitions and events on a grand scale and usually include:

✱ Conference rooms and meeting rooms

✱ Registration and welcome areas

✱ Box office services for public events

✱ Good transport access – road, rail and air

✱ Car parking facilities

✱ Support services for exhibitors and event organisers

✱ Food and catering facilities

✱ Adequate toilet facilities

✱ Easy access for visitors with special needs

✱ Nearby hotel accommodation.

Madison Square Garden in New York describes itself as the world's most famous arena. It first opened in May 1879 but has been rebuilt four times. It combines 76,178 square metres (820,000 square feet) of indoor space which includes a 20,000 seat arena, a 5600 seat theatre and a 3344 square metres (36,000 square feet) exposition rotunda. It is home to the New York Knicks basketball team and the New York Rangers ice hockey team. Seating arrangements vary between events. Such events include concerts, basketball, ice hockey, wrestling, boxing, tennis, the Ringling Brothers Circus, horse shows, ice shows, track and field events. For further information visit http://www.thegarden.com

Historic buildings

Historic buildings include stately homes, castles, royal palaces, birthplaces and houses of famous people. They have been adapted to allow tourists to visit, have improved health and safety features and incorporated additional tourist facilities such as guides, toilets and souvenir shops. Historic buildings help visitors understand the history and culture of the country they are visiting.

CASE STUDY

Versailles, France

The Palace of Versailles is one of the most famous historic buildings in Europe, with three chateaux and extensive gardens. It was originally built as a hunting lodge in 1624 and became the royal palace of King Louis XIV. Until 1789 it remained the seat of the monarchy in France and its design reflects its power and wealth. The buildings contain 700 rooms and 67 staircases, highly decorated and beautifully preserved. The most popular attraction is the Hall of Mirrors, a magnificent room that was the focus of grand celebrations and royal marriages. The parkland covers some 800 hectares and includes over 200,000 trees.

The royal palace is also historically significant as the place where Germany signed the Treaty of Versailles in 1919 to signify the end of the First World War and claim responsibility for the lives lost.

The Royal Palace of Versailles in France

Complete the following table with details of one historic building in Europe and one in North America:

	HISTORIC BUILDING IN EUROPE	HISTORIC BUILDING IN NORTH AMERICA
Name		
Location		
Main attractions		
Important events that took place		

Ancient monuments and historic monuments

An *ancient monument* or *historic monument* is a site that was built before the end of the Western Roman Empire, 476 AD, and represents a good example of the past.

Monuments can include:

* Buildings
* Forts
* Burial grounds
* Henges
* Stone circles
* Field systems
* Mines
* Hilltop enclosures
* Villas
* Roads.

One of the most visited ancient or historic monuments in Europe is the Roman town of Pompeii in southern Italy. In AD 79 Mount Vesuvius erupted burying the town of Pompeii. The remains were discovered in 1750, including

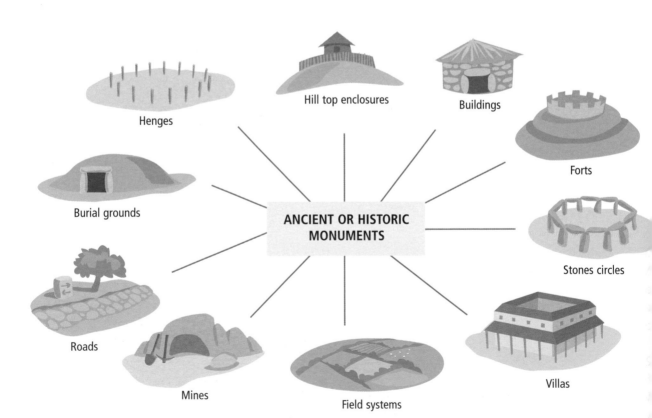

Figure 3.6 *Ancient or historic monuments are among the most popular tourist attractions*

buildings, temples and the remains of people who lived there. Excavations are on display in the National Archaeological Museum in Naples, including colourful paintings and mosaics. The buildings in Pompeii are very well preserved, including the Forum, the centre of civic and religious functions, the gladiators' barracks, theatres and many fine houses.

Skills practice

1 Locate and describe an ancient monument in Europe. Why is it popular with visitors?

2 Locate and describe an ancient monument in North America. Why is it popular with visitors?

3 Suggest why it is more difficult to locate an ancient monument in America than in Europe.

Think about it

Over 2.5 million people visit Pompeii each year. Why do you think this is such an interesting place to visit?

The Forum at Pompeii, Italy

Museums and art galleries

Millions of people visit *museums and art galleries* every year to view and interact with exhibits which give an insight into the culture and history of a destination.

The Louvre in central Paris houses, amongst 29,000 pieces of art and artefacts, the world's most famous painting, the *Mona Lisa*, and the statue *Venus de Milo*. Approximately six million people visit the Louvre each year. The building was first used to exhibit artefacts in 1793, making it one of the earliest European museums. The Louvre is easily recognised by its glass pyramid entrance.

The Museum of Modern Art (MoMA), New York, was founded in 1929 as an educational institution and dedicates itself to being the foremost museum of modern art in the world. Over 1.5 million people visit MoMA each year. It has over 135,000 paintings, sculptures, architectural models, drawings, prints, photographs and over 19,000 films and four million film stills.

The Louvre in Paris is one of the world's great museums and art galleries

Tourist facilities

There are many *tourist facilities* that are designed to meet the needs of visitors. These include:

* Accommodation
* Food and drink
* Entertainment
* Events.

Accommodation

The *range of accommodation* available at a tourist destination varies according to the quality and level of service on offer and also the price of stay. Some visitors prefer the independence of self-catering accommodation, whereas others like varying levels of service and luxury in the type of establishment they choose. Levels of service can be classified into bed and breakfast stays; half board, where an evening meal is provided in the cost; full board, which includes lunch and evening meal; and all-inclusive, which adds bar snacks and drinks to the full board option.

The main *types of accommodation* on offer can include: hotels, guesthouses, inns, holiday centres, hostels, villas, apartments, chalets, caravans, camping, and farm accommodation. Each of these appeals to different types of tourist and so many destinations will seek to provide a range of accommodation types to attract a cross-section of holidaymaker. Disabled groups and the elderly may seek accommodation that has good access. Young families may wish to have family rooms that are adjacent to the main bedroom and be in accommodation that welcomes family groups. Backpackers and students who are travelling tend to seek cheaper accommodation with fewer facilities.

A hotel tends to have five or more bedrooms that are available to let but not calling itself a guesthouse or a boarding house. A guesthouse is a modern name for a boarding house, a private house where the owner rents out rooms and may also provide meals. An inn or public house may have a small number of guest bedrooms that tend to be advertised on a bed-and-breakfast basis.

Farm accommodation has become a familiar sight in the countryside as farmers offer rooms and farm cottages to tourists. It is an attractive alternative for those who wish to stay in the countryside. Not only can they witness rural life at first hand but also stay in authentic farm accommodation.

Caravans and camping range from a basic farm field to purpose-built sites with restaurants, bars, shops, children's activities and other on-site services.

Think about it

What are the advantages and disadvantages of camping?

Holiday centres are often built for the purpose of catering for large numbers of tourists and have become resorts in their own right. They include an all-inclusive package of accommodation, food and entertainment.

The UK company Haven Europe operates 30 holiday parcs in France, Italy and Spain. In 22 locations they rent spaces in locally managed parcs to provide luxury mobile homes and camping facilities. In addition they own 8 French Siblu (pronounced 'see blue') holiday parcs in the popular tourist regions of Aquitaine, Brittany, Charente Maritime, Languedoc and Vendee.

Skills practice

Using a range of travel brochures and travel guides compare the variety, cost and standard of accommodation in an American city with a rural holiday in a European destination.

Food and drink

Food and drink can be associated with specific countries, regions and places. When we travel abroad we expect to see traditional foods on the menu. Eating locally prepared food is part of the tourist experience of visiting another country. Very often we are attracted to a particular country because we like the local food and drink. Many destinations choose to offer a range of international and local food and drink to meet the needs of a wide range of tourists.

Two areas of tourism that are growing in popularity are food and wine tourism. This includes tourists being offered experiences and visits which solely focus on the food or wine produced in a particular area.

CASE STUDY

Napa Valley, California

Napa Valley is 30 miles long and up to five miles wide and is famous for its wine production. It attracts 5 million visitors a year, with a peak in the number of visitors during the harvest months of September and October. There are over 200 wineries in Napa Valley and it has become one of California's most popular visitor destinations. The valley's warm climate and rich fertile soil has made the area perfect for growing vines. The region is famous for growing grape varieties that are traditionally found in the Bordeaux region of France, with a recent trend to growing Italian varieties. Many tourist industries have developed as a result of the vineyards; these include hot air balloon rides, private visits to wineries and wine tours by bicycle and by kayak along the river . There are many quality restaurants that are popular with visitors.
For more information visit:
http://www.napavalley.com
http://www.nappavalleyonline.com

Wine tours are popular in France and Italy and also in other countries in central and southern Europe. What are the attractions in going to visit a winery? What type of tourist is attracted to these places?

Complete the following table, the first two have been done for you.

FOOD AND DRINK	COUNTRY OR REGION IT IS ASSOCIATED WITH
Pizza	Italy
Champagne	France
Pasta	
Black Forest Gateau	
Strudel	
Hamburger	
Paella	
Goulash	
Tapas	
Souvlaki	
Camembert	
Chowder	

Entertainment

Entertainment plays an important role in the attraction to visit a particular destination. Some tourists go to a particular place solely for the entertainment on offer; others seek amusement once they have arrived. The entertainment available can take on a variety of forms and will appeal to a range of ages and types of visitor. It can include: theatre, cinema, music, comedy, sport, street performers, nightclubs, pubs and bars. Each of these entertainment categories can also be divided into different aspects which will appeal to different visitors, for example music can mean experiencing live music such as classical, opera, musicals, pop and rock concerts; participating in music in karaoke sessions, and hearing recorded music in pubs and nightclubs.

Large cities will offer many types of entertainment as a focus for a range of tourists, and such entertainment can sometimes be found concentrated within particular areas, for example theatre districts. Tourist resorts can also offer a range of entertainment to visitors or specialise in certain types of entertainment, and hotels can also play their role in providing a programme of activities to keep guests entertained.

CASE STUDY
Broadway, New York

Broadway, the famous theatre district in New York, is located within a thin strip of Manhattan, called the Great White Way. There are 38 theatres packed into this small area of the city, most of which host world famous productions each night. Broadway theatres offer large-scale productions with professional and well-known actors and actresses.

Off-Broadway theatre offers a wider variety of styles, presenting work that mainstream Broadway is concerned will not make lots of money. Smaller venues with 100–500 seats are classified as Off-Broadway.

As well as the plays and musicals available on Broadway, visitors to New York can also apply for tickets to be part of the audience for the recording or broadcast of approximately 30 regular television shows.

CASE STUDY
Ibiza

The Mediterranean island of Ibiza has become increasingly popular as a holiday destination during the past ten years due to its reputation as being the centre of the world's clubbing scene, which dominates three months of the year.

Many clubs and resorts on the island have gained international status for the DJs and music on offer. Famous clubs include Café del

Mar, Pacha and Space. The island is advertised as the summer party capital of the world.

The island doesn't only offer clubs and music, it also provides the traditional Mediterranean attractions of warm climate, sandy beaches, history and a wide range of holiday accommodation, food and entertainment. Ibiza tourism officials have recognised that 65 per cent of visitors return for at least a second time, although they recognise the difficulty in trying to attract new tourists to the island because of its reputation as a summer party capital.

worn and jugglers, mime acts, acrobats and fire-eaters crowd the narrow streets.

Skills practice

1 Describe one major event in either Europe or North America.

2 Why does it attract large numbers of people?

3 How does a town or city benefit from hosting such an event?

Think about it

What entertainments and events interest you when you are going on holiday? Is this the same as your friends and family? How does a tourist destination try and cater for tourists with different needs?

Travel times to different destinations, the significance of time zones and the International Date Line

Think about it

Why is it important to know the departure time of a journey and also how long the journey will take?

Events

Events can provide the main attraction to a particular destination and appeal to a wide range of audiences. They are organised and designed to attract large numbers of people. They include sporting events, music festivals, art festivals and carnivals and may range from international ones to local ones:

✱ International events are important to the global community, for example the Olympic Games where athletes from across the globe compete against each other.

✱ National events are important to a whole country, for example the Celtic music festival, Dublin, to celebrate the musical history of Ireland.

✱ Regional events are important to the region of a country, for example the Texas Hot and Spicy festival celebrating the food of the region.

✱ Local events are important to a village, town or immediate locality, for example the Venice Carnival, Italy, where traditional masks are

Time zones

When we travel to different countries we may pass across different *time zones*, which means having to change our watches and clocks to local time as we pass through those countries.

Imagine that the earth is like an orange, where imaginary lines extend from the north to the south poles like segments of the orange. The most important line is the prime meridian that is used as the starting point; the most often used is the Greenwich Meridian that passes through London. Meridians are used to calculate distances west or east of the meridian and these are called longitudes. When the Sun is at its highest position at midday (noon), all places along the same line of longitude experience midday.

As the Earth turns from west to east, places on its surface turn from morning to noon, afternoon, evening and night. To the west it is before midday and east it is after midday. When it is midday in London it is 7 am in New York and 1 pm in Paris.

Countries like France and Great Britain have the same time zone for the entire country.

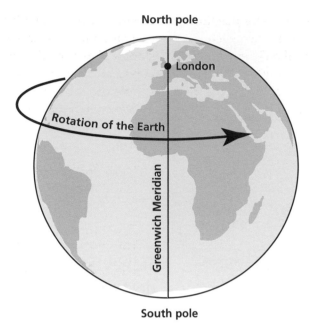

Figure 3.7 The Greenwich Meridian

However, larger countries like America and Canada extend across several time zones. When it is 7 am in New York it is 4am in California.

International Date Line

By moving further west along the map between the western edge of North America and Russia,

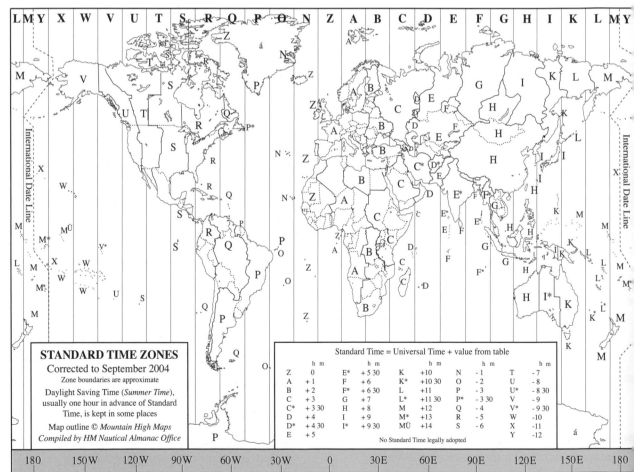

STANDARD TIME ZONES
Corrected to September 2004
Zone boundaries are approximate

Daylight Saving Time (*Summer Time*),
usually one hour in advance of Standard
Time, is kept in some places

Map outline © *Mountain High Maps*
Compiled by HM Nautical Almanac Office

Standard Time = Universal Time + value from table

	h m		h m		h m		h m		h m
Z	0	E*	+ 5 30	K	+10	N	- 1	T	- 7
A	+ 1	F	+ 6	K*	+10 30	O	- 2	U	- 8
B	+ 2	F*	+ 6 30	L	+11	P	- 3	U*	- 8 30
C	+ 3	G	+ 7	L*	+11 30	P*	- 3 30	V	- 9
C*	+ 3 30	H	+ 8	M	+12	Q	- 4	V*	- 9 30
D	+ 4	I	+ 9	M*	+13	R	- 5	W	-10
D*	+ 4 30	I*	+ 9 30	MÜ	+14	S	- 6	X	-11
E	+ 5							Y	-12

No Standard Time legally adopted

Figure 3.8 World time zones

there comes a point where places along this line of longitude are 12 hours behind the Greenwich Meridian. If it is midday along the Greenwich Meridian it is midnight along this other line, called the *International Date Line*. Moving further west would not only be an earlier time but also a different day.

The International Date Line avoids crossing through any country. It would create problems to be in the same country with parts of it in totally different days of the week.

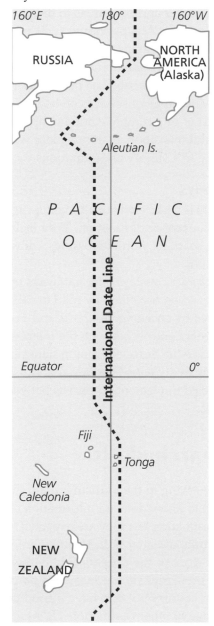

Figure 3.9 International Date Line

People travelling by air between long-haul destinations can cross several time zones before reaching their destination. They may lose or gain several hours. This interferes with their body clock and as such they may feel the need to sleep at odd hours of the day. This is called 'jet lag'. People are often tired after travelling and losing or gaining hours can often lead to temporary fatigue.

Skills practice

Complete the following table. You will need to refer to Figure 3.8 and an atlas. The first one has been done for you.

The time in London is 12 pm
The time in New York is 7 am

The time in Paris is 12 pm
The time in New York is _____

The time in Berlin is 8 pm
The time in Paris is _____

The time in Dallas is 2 am
The time in Boston is _____

The time in Los Angeles is 6 pm
The time in Montreal _____

The time in Washington DC is 10 am
The time in Reykjavik _____

The time in Madrid is 2 pm
The time in Athens is _____

The time in Budapest is 9 pm
The time in Vancouver is _____

The time in Amsterdam is 5 am
The time in Helsinki is _____

The time in Copenhagen is 8 am
The time in New York is_____

The time in Chicago is 4 pm
The time in Rome is _____

Key terms

Time zone The world is divided into zones of time, so that as you travel east you gain time and as you travel west you lose time.

International Date Line This is an imaginary line that runs north to south at 180° longitude, either side of which the time difference is 12 hours. So, if it is midday along the Greenwich Meridian it is midnight along the International Date Line.

The main travel routes and gateways to major destinations

Travel routes

Travel routes include road, rail, air and sea. Each of these are chosen depending on distance to travel, cost, convenience and availability, length of journey time and services available whilst travelling.

Road travel involves cars and coaches journeying along motorways, autobahns, freeways, trunk roads and through tunnels. Road travel tends to be mainly for domestic tourism and short visits over international borders. Using a car offers flexibility in terms of choosing route, time of departure and time of arrival. A driver can choose to break a journey with stops en-route or drive straight through to a destination. Coach travel tends to be less flexible as pick-up and drop-off points need to be established and there is a larger group of people to transfer to the final destination. Coaches and taxis can also be used to transport passengers from airports to their holiday destination – this is known as a *transfer*.

Rail travel offers high-speed links between major destinations as well as regional links and also some scenic railway routes. Rail companies can offer a range of services, including different seating accommodation, buffet cars and refreshment services, and a range of ticket types depending on the time and type of journey.

Air travel is the fastest method of travel available to a destination and can be used for domestic, short-haul and long-haul journeys. As a form of travel flying has increased in popularity over the past ten years with the result that there are now more airlines offering flights and there are price wars between airlines. Low-cost airlines, for example, offer cheaper seats with a reduced level of in-flight service.

There are two types of air travel, *scheduled flights*, which follow a particular timetable and fly whether or not the seats are all filled, and *charter flights*, which are linked with package holidays. These are when an aircraft is booked by tour operators for a certain destination at a certain time; they do not follow a regular timetable.

Travelling by air allows a quicker journey time and the opportunity to travel over long distances with relative ease; in addition there are in-flight services of refreshment and duty free sales on offer. As with rail travel the passengers are restricted to specific travel times for departure and arrival; they also have the disadvantage of having to check-in for their flight usually two hours before departure, which adds to journey time.

Sea travel subdivides into two types, ferries and cruises. *Ferry* transport takes travellers on foot, in cars, lorries and coaches across stretches of water and offers services such as shops, restaurants, cabins, lounges and play areas to the passengers. Other types of vessel providing such a service include sea catamarans.

Cruises on the other hand involve large ships, which are often described as floating hotels and offer a wide range of services on board. They tend to be part of or a complete holiday option offering luxury and relaxation all in one place while travelling to a variety of destinations.

Gateways

A *gateway* is a place where a traveller can enter or leave a country or destination. They include airports, seaports, border crossings, railway and bus stations.

Land border crossings offer gateways to other countries when travelling by road or rail and are monitored by checking passports and visas. Since 1995 border controls between the member countries of the European Union who signed the Schengen Treaty have been relaxed, causing unrestricted movement of tourists between these countries.

Research skills

People working in the tourism industry cannot be expected to know detailed information about every destination but they are expected to demonstrate research skills to obtain information for their work or their clients. Some travel and tourism professionals specialise in a particular region or country but also have a good general knowledge of other destinations. It is expected that you can identify important destinations and attractions but would need to research opening times or latest prices.

Researching involves:

* being clear about what you are trying to find out

* knowing how to search for information

* deciding what might be useful

* collecting and presenting relevant information

* drawing conclusions about your findings

* acknowledging your sources.

Being clear about what you are trying to find out

Setting clear aims and objectives is important when beginning any form of research, whether it be designing a questionnaire or finding information in a library or on the Internet. The *aim* is what you intend to find out or write about. The *objectives* are the steps you are going to take in order to meet your aim.

The following is an example:

Aim:

To discover information about the location of a destination, its landscape and climate.

Objectives:

* To select a suitable travel destination

* To research information on a selected travel destination

* To identify and describe its location

* To identify the main features of its landscape and identify major landscape features

* To identify main features of its climate using climate data.

Knowing how to search for information

It is important to get to know how a library is organised. There is usually a catalogue or a computer system that tells you what books are on the shelves and which ones are being borrowed. These computer systems are searchable using a title or author search or a key word search.

If you are using the Internet then knowing how to search for information will save you a lot of time.

It is best to start with one search engine such as Google although others are available.

A *Boolean search* allows you to use certain key words; they may differ between search engines although the basic principles are the same:

AND will let you add terms together (e.g. Spain AND Holiday).

OR widens the search to look for either word (e.g. Mallorca OR Majorca).

NOT allows you to exclude related words (e.g. Turkey AND Holiday NOT Birds).

Deciding what might be useful

It is easy to become interested in a topic and try to cover too much information. Find out who your audience is and remove information that is irrelevant no matter how interesting it may appear. Knowing who is likely to read or hear your work will tell you something about what level of information you require

Collecting and presenting relevant information

Try to collect information from a variety of different sources as this will help to make your findings more reliable. If possible support your evidence from another source. Information can change very quickly and as such you need to be sure that you have the most accurate and up-to-date information.

Drawing conclusions about your findings

If you have researched a lot of information and have many maps, tables and graphs in your report then it is useful to provide a summary and be able to draw conclusions about your findings.

Acknowledging your sources

Whatever books and resources you have been using always quote them in your writing. This is useful if you want to come back to a source to add more detail or to let the reader know where to find further information. It is also important if you are copying information to quote the source. You would feel cheated if someone copied your work without permission; copying other people's work without referencing it is called *plagiarism*.

After writing a quote in speech marks, place the author and date in brackets with the relevant page number separated by a comma. For example,

'Customer needs and expectations are constantly changing' (Marvell 2003, p. 53).

At the end of your assignments you need to include a list of references. They should be arranged alphabetically. If the same author is used then the most recent date is used first.

The correct way of acknowledging and referencing sources is to use the Harvard style of referencing:

Author, Author initials. (Date) *Title*. Place of publication: Publisher.

The title should be underlined or placed in *italics*, for example:

Marvell, A. (2003) *UK Travel Destinations*. Oxford: Heinemann Educational Publishers.

In journals or newspapers where there are many authors, the style is the following:

Author, Author initials. (Date) Title of article. *Title of journal*, volume (part number) or date, page numbers.

An example is:

Holden, W. (2005) Hidden gems of townhouse Paris. *The Mail on Sunday*, 1 May, pp. 92–93.

When using Internet sites try to quote the author and date of publication if at all possible, or the date accessed, for example:

Little, M. (2004) Freelance Spain. A brief history of Spain, 17 November, http://www.spainview.com/history.html

Primary sources

Primary sources refer to reports or published first-hand information. For example, an airport requires information about the quality of services that are offered. It is only possible to gather this information by asking customers directly. The responses may then be analysed and presented in a report, which is then used to inform decision-making.

Secondary sources

It is an important skill to be able to gather information about destinations from a range of *secondary sources*, including gazetteers; the Internet; brochures; maps; guidebooks; newspapers and trade journals.

It is essential to know which source to select to develop research skills and also to recognise that the sources must be precise, valid and provide a suitable amount of detail. Knowing which sources to choose allows efficient information gathering that will save time.

Gazetteers are published geographical dictionaries or indexes, which contain a list of geographical features and descriptions organised in alphabetical order.

The *Internet* is a popular source for a huge range of information and many tourist boards and visitor attractions have dedicated websites to provide information to visitors.

Brochures are produced in order to promote a range of products and services including holidays and accommodation.

Maps provide the location of geographical features and can include road maps and other travel routes, street maps, and maps suitable for walking and hiking.

Guidebooks are produced to provide information about a particular destination or area and contain a variety of information on the main visitor attractions, history, places of interest to visit, culture, sport and accommodation in the locality.

Newspapers report information on destinations as items of news. Some national newspapers publish regular travel supplements that provide details about travel destinations.

Trade journals are publications devoted to news and features designed to inform members of the industry. Examples of trade journals for travel and tourism include *Travel Weekly* and *Travel Trade Gazette*.

Primary sources Collecting information first-hand, such as from surveys and from interviewing people.

Secondary sources These are sources that have already been published, such as the Internet, brochures, books, newspapers.

1 Find an example of a secondary source from the following list:
   - Gazetteers
   - Internet
   - Brochures
   - Maps
   - Guide books
   - Newspapers
   - Trade journals.

2 Write out the author, date of publication, title, place of publication and publisher as you expect to see it written in a list of references.

3 Briefly write out a description of what information the source contains.

4 Identify the intended audience.

5 Describe an example of a primary source and how you might use it in your research.

Tourist generating and receiving areas

Tourist generating areas are countries where people travel from and *tourist receiving areas* are those areas where people travel to. People who visit travel destinations are described as *inbound tourists*. There were 400 million inbound tourists to European countries in 2002, representing 57 per cent of global travel. Asia and the Pacific received the second largest numbers of inbound tourists. The Americas received the third largest with 16 per cent of all inbound tourists.

Those tourists who leave their country to travel to another are described as *outbound tourists*.

Tourist appeal

There are many reasons why people visit principal destinations as inbound tourists. This is due to the appeal of the destination in meeting the needs of different types of tourists. The appeal of these destinations is reflected within holiday brochures and guidebooks. It is easy to see the differences when comparing an 18–30-year-old's holiday brochure with a summer sun brochure and a brochure specialising in holidays for mature couples and the retired.

Some destinations can appeal to a wide range of tourists and combine many different types of attractions. For example, in Austria walking holidays and Sound of Music tours are advertised alongside activity holidays, extreme sports, skiing holidays and city breaks.

Future popularity and appeal of tourist destinations

There are a number of factors that have a direct impact on the *future popularity and appeal of tourist destinations*. These are:

* Advances in technology
* Major events
* Security
* Exchange rates
* Promotional activity
* Fashion.

Advances in technology

The growth in home computers has revolutionised communication and access to information. Through developments in e-tourism people are able to book holidays using the Internet and use computers to research information regarding a visitor destination.

Tour operators, tourist boards, hotels, theme parks and local authorities are able to provide a great amount of information via the Internet. Details of events, attractions, accommodation, weather conditions and transport can help a tourist plan a holiday. Some Internet sites have

1 Using a range of holiday brochures that appeal to different types of tourists, compare the differences in expectation of a family group going on holiday, a recently retired couple and a group of university students by completing the following table:

FACTORS	NEEDS OF A FAMILY GROUP	NEEDS OF A RETIRED COUPLE	NEEDS OF A GROUP OF UNIVERSITY STUDENTS
Climate			
Topography			
Natural attractions			
Built attractions			
Events			
Food, drink and entertainment			
Accommodation available			
Accessibility and types or transport			

2 Identify the similarities and differences between the three groups.

become very sophisticated in offering virtual tours of destinations, attractions and hotels.

Advances in technology related to transport usually mean that more passengers are able to travel quicker and cheaper than before. The Airbus A380 is a brand new 'double decker' aircraft that seats 555 passengers. The wings were designed in the UK and the aeroplane is being assembled in France with assistance from Germany and Spain. As it is a wide-bodied aircraft it can be adapted to offer in-flight beds, and there is also dedicated space within the aircraft for a diverse range of uses, and could potentially include office space, shop, bar and even a mini-casino. It is expected to go into service in 2006.

1 Using the Internet take a virtual tour of a theme park, hotel or destination in Europe or North America.

2 What did you learn during your tour?

3 What advantage does a virtual tour have over a traditional guidebook or brochure?

Airbus 380

Major events

Major events such as international sporting events, festivals and exhibitions can attract tourists from all over the world. Not only does the event encourage people to visit but international media provides an opportunity to promote a country as a potential tourist destination and also to encourage repeat visits by tourists who have visited before.

The UEFA European Championship is the third-largest sporting event in the world, after the Football World Cup and the Olympics. The event held in 2000, called Euro 2000, was hosted by Holland and Belgium. It attracted 1.2 million football spectators and broadcast to a global television audience of 7 billion viewers.

Major events can also highlight less popular towns and cities. For example, the Barcelona Olympic Games in 1992 helped to provide an alternative tourist destination to the Spanish Costas and enabled the city to become one of the top European city-break destinations.

Think about it

What international sporting or music events have you watched on television? Did it encourage you to think about visiting the countries they were held in or travelling to see a similar event?

Security

Security is one of the key issues when considering the impact on the future popularity and appeal of a destination. Tourists need to feel safe and confident about visiting a destination; if they do not feel safe then it is unlikely that they will visit.

The terrorist attacks on the United States on September 11th 2001 had a dramatic effect on the numbers of inbound visitors. The terrorist attacks were particularly disturbing as passenger aircraft were used as weapons. This reduced the numbers of people wishing to travel long distances as people preferred to stay closer to home.

The wars in Afghanistan and Iraq and terrorist attacks in Bali and Egypt further reduced consumer confidence in long-haul travel and countries such as the United States experienced a decline in inbound tourists from the UK. The US Office of Travel and Tourism Industries and the Department of Commerce recorded 3.8 million arrivals from the UK in 2002. This represents a decline of 7 per cent on the 4.1 million UK visitors in 2001. The numbers of visitors include people travelling on business, visiting friends and relatives (VFR), as well as holidaymakers.

Further concerns over personal safety relating to the infectious disease SARS (Severe Acute Respiratory Syndrome) in 2002 and 2003 reduced the numbers of UK visitors travelling to the Far East and to Canada.

Governments and the travel industry have reassured tourists that they are doing their best to maximise security. Reduced fares and promotions have also helped consumer confidence to recover.

Outbound holiday visits by UK tourists between 1999 and 2002 saw a 29 per cent decline in visits to North America, an 11 per cent rise in the number of tourists to destinations of member countries of the European Union and a 16 per cent rise in the number of visits to European countries outside of the European Union.

Advice on travel safety and security is issued by the Foreign and Commonwealth Office via their website and is updated several times daily. For further information visit http://www.fco.gov.uk

Skills practice

1 Describe the impact of international security issues on passengers travelling from the UK.

2 Visit the Foreign and Commonwealth Office website and examine the advice given to UK residents travelling to destinations in Europe and North America.

Exchange rates

The *exchange rate* or value of the British pound in relation to other currencies can affect the popularity of tourist destinations. When the value of the British pound is higher than other currencies it makes travelling abroad less expensive as we are receiving more local currency for our money. When the value of the British pound is low compared to other currencies it makes travelling abroad more expensive as we are receiving less local currency for our money. Values of foreign currency are displayed in travel agents, where there is a bureau de change, in banks and newspapers.

Some countries within the European Union have replaced their traditional currency with the Euro. The Euro was launched in January 1999 and enables tourists and businesses to trade between countries using the same currency. There are twelve countries that have the single currency: Austria, Belgium, Finland, France, Germany, Greece, Ireland, Italy, Luxembourg, Netherlands, Portugal and Spain.

Each time money is exchanged, a bureau de change or bank charges a small commission fee. Although some offer commission-free exchanges where no charge is made, the amount of commission is usually hidden in the rate of exchange.

Exchange rates are not the only consideration when calculating the cost of goods and services abroad. The *rate of inflation* is an important factor as this shows how much prices have increased. If a holiday destination is seen to be expensive or offer poor value for money then cheaper alternative destinations are usually chosen.

Skills practice

1 Using today's exchange rates make a list of those currencies that have seen an increase in value and those that have seen a decrease in value.

2 To what extent does this have an impact on the popularity of the destinations?

3 Which of these currencies are in Europe and North America?

Promotional activity

How a destination is promoted can have a major impact on its popularity and appeal. Local authorities and national tourist boards spend thousands of pounds each year to market their destination to attract inbound tourism. It is important that potential visitors know what the destination can offer in terms of accommodation, facilities and attractions.

Most other countries have a national tourist board office in London in order to promote their country to the UK and to offer advice and travel

TOURIST CURRENCY RATES OF EXCHANGE	
Australia (dollar)	2.3514
Barbados (dollar)	3.3474
Canada (dollar)	2.2403
China (renminbi)	15.16
Czech (koruna)	40.94
Cyprus (pound)	0.8220
Egypt (pound)	9.7309
Euro	1.4119
Hong Kong (dollar)	14.15
India (rupee)	73.44
Indonesia (rupiah)	15702
Japan (yen)	199.41
Kenya (shilling)	129.90
Malta (lira)	0.6064
Mexico (peso)	19.00
Morocco (dirham)	15.30
New Zealand (dollar)	2.5115
South Africa (rand)	11.13
Sri Lanka (rupee)	176.49
Switzerland (franc)	2.2023
Thailand (bath)	68.31
Tunisia (dinar)	2.1626
Turkey (new lira)	2.4364
United States (dollar)	1.8277

One way of keeping in touch with the current tourist currency rates is through the business pages of daily newspapers. The above is a selection of rates for the British pound recorded in the press on 11 April 2005

services to UK residents who are interested in their country as a travel destination.

The European Union is the main tourist generating and receiving area for international tourism flows. On 1 May 2004 ten new countries joined the EU: Cyprus, Czech Republic, Estonia, Hungary, Latvia, Lithuania, Malta, Poland,

Slovakia and Slovenia. Further countries are set to join, including Bulgaria, Romania and Turkey. These provide new market opportunities to attract inbound tourists. Malta and Cyprus are already popular tourist destinations and countries like Hungary are working hard to promote themselves to attract tourists from the UK.

CASE STUDY

Hungary

The Hungarian Tourist Board recognises that Eastern Europeans are familiar with what Hungary has to offer, while Western Europeans know very little. The Tourist Board has to change the perception of Hungary as an Eastern European country to one that is recognised as a fellow European country. In the UK the Hungarian Tourist Board organised a series of promotions based on '2004 Year of Hungarian Culture'. City breaks to Budapest were promoted in Germany, the UK and Belgium. Current campaigns focus on health tourism, as Budapest is Europe's largest spa city with 80 thermal springs and 20 spa baths. Promotional channels include billboards, posters in travel agents, advertisements in the press and on television, including CNN, CNBC, Eurosport, National Geographic and the Travel Channel.

Source: Mintel (2004)

Skills practice

Using a range of newspapers, travel supplements and magazines provide examples of European and North American destinations that are advertising their country or destination in order to attract more visitors from the UK.

Fashion

Changing fashions will affect the popularity of destinations as one resort becomes increasingly popular in comparison to another. *Fashions* can be defined as a current style adopted by society. Fashions are affected by technological change, media influences, new developments and changing customer expectations, as well as employment trends and amount of personal income. Fashionable destinations tend to be visited more frequently than those that are not.

Fashions can be reflected in social trends and attitudes. New types of holidays are created by changes in fashion, which in turn creates changes in demand. A growing interest in health and sport has generated a rise in the number of specialist activity holidays, including underwater diving, golf, spa holidays, water sports, horse riding and mountain biking. Not only do these holidays offer a chance to relax but also to learn new skills, meet other people with similar interests and to further personal achievement.

Key terms

Tourist generating areas These are areas where tourists travel from.

Tourist receiving areas These are areas where tourists travel to.

Outbound travel Those who leave one country to travel to another country.

Inbound travel Those who arrive in one country from another country.

Exchange rate The value of one currency against other currencies.

Rate of inflation The rate at which prices increase in an economy.

Different types of transport

Tourists may have choices to make relating to the type of *transport*. For example, they may be able to choose between different departure airports if they are flying. They can also choose between different airlines, as many European destinations are accessible by both traditional airlines and 'low-cost' airlines, scheduled and charter services.

Tourists can also choose to travel by Eurostar and other high-speed rail networks. Alternatively, people can choose to drive to their destination using ferries or the Channel Tunnel and the autoroute or motorway system.

The methods by which tourists may choose to travel are:

* Road
* Rail
* Air
* Sea.

Road

When travelling by road, tourists can choose to travel by car or by coach. Travel by road is the most popular form of transport in Europe, carrying 78 per cent of passengers. Even when alternatives are presented, the car is the most accessible form of transport over short distances. Car use is more popular with domestic holidays but the use of ferry services and Eurotunnel have provided access to the European motorway system. Motorway networks are fast and efficient although drivers are sometimes discouraged from driving into major towns and cities. Concerns over pollution and congestion have meant that most city authorities have invested in other forms of public transport such as park-and-ride schemes.

Car hire is widely available and tourists can rent vehicles from airports, rail terminals, seaports and also through accommodation providers, as well as booking directly through a car hire company. Fly-drive holidays are very popular in North America, however many rental companies in North America require that drivers carry a major credit card, have a valid license and are over the age of 21.

European motorways display two numbers, a motorway or autoroute number and an E number, identified by green and white signs. The European International Network is a series of numbered routes across Europe and consists of a grid system of road numbers, with even numbers used for routes running east to west and odd numbers running north to south. The idea is to simplify the use of road numbers, which can change when crossing country borders. However, not all European countries have adopted the system as many major routes have been designated as E roads in the UK, but few, if any, are signposted using this system.

Most motorways or autoroutes in Europe and North America are toll roads and most bridges also demand payment in order to cross.

When driving abroad it is important to be aware of driving regulations as they differ from country to country. For example, in France the maximum speed permitted on a motorway is 130 km/hr (81 mph) and 110 km/hr (69 mph) when wet or for drivers holding a licence for less than two years. In towns the legal maximum is 50 km/hr (31 mph).

Skills practice

Using a European road atlas or a route planner on the Internet, identify the E roads used on the following journeys:

Paris to Amsterdam

Rome to Amsterdam

Paris to Munich

Bordeaux to Toulouse

Le Mans to Calais

Madrid to Valencia

Nancy to Salzburg

Hamburg to Berlin

Tromsø to Tornio

Budapest to Gdansk

Skills practice

You need to do research to answer the following questions.

1 What are the driving laws in the USA and Canada?

2 How do they compare to Europe and the UK?

Outbound *coach tourism* is dominated by UK trips to France, usually for four nights or more. The amount of coaches travelling between the UK and France is growing at a rate of 3.5 per cent each year. In 2002, 219,460 coaches travelled between the UK and France either using the Dover–Calais route or Eurotunnel. Other popular destinations that have seen a rise in the numbers of coaches from the UK include Belgium, Italy and Luxembourg, with Central and Eastern European destinations growing in importance.

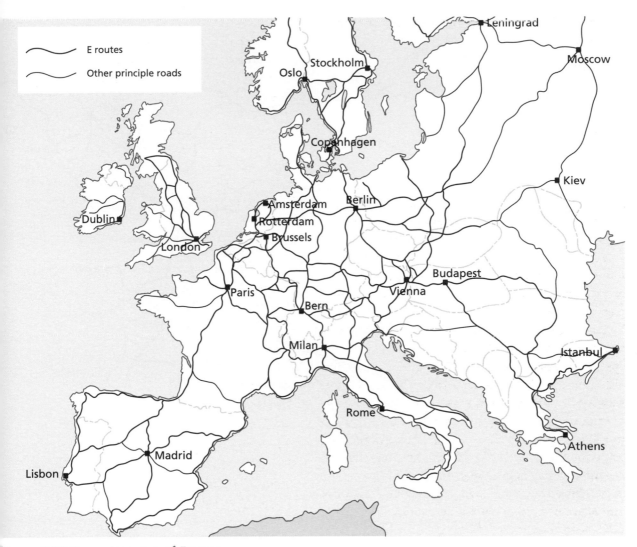

Figure 3.10 Key autoroutes of Europe

The top five coach holiday destinations in Europe as booked by UK tourists through Leger Holidays are:

1. France
2. Belgium
3. Italy
4. Austria
5. Holland.

Source: Travel Weekly (2002)

The two largest UK coach operators are Shearings and Wallace Arnold. Shearings carries approximately 575,000 passengers a year, owns 38 hotels and a fleet of 259 coaches. Wallace Arnold carries around 550,000 passengers a year with a fleet of 225 coaches and owns 8 hotels. The coach routes follow the autoroutes (Figure 3.10).

Travel within Europe is dominated by Eurolines, a European network of coach companies that was established to coordinate coach services across several countries. The company serves over 300 cities and 500 destinations.

In North America, Greyhound is the most established long-distance bus company, offering routes to all of the major cities in the USA as well as the Canadian cities of Montreal, Toronto and Vancouver. Bus routes follow the interstate highways (Figure 3.11) and stop every 100 miles to pick up passengers and to stop for comfort breaks and to change drivers. Buses are the cheapest way to travel long distance and are favoured by budget travellers.

Coaches are also used to *transfer* people between the destination and the resort. Tour operators hire local coach companies to pick up passengers at airports and drop them off en-route. Taxis can also be used to transport smaller numbers of people.

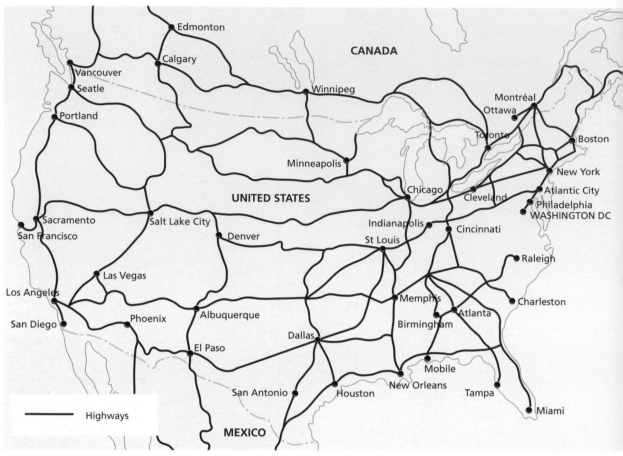

Figure 3.11 Key highways of North America

Rail

The *railway network* in Europe covers some 154,000 kilometres (95,500 miles) compared to the motorway network which covers 50,000 kilometres (31,000 miles). Despite such a vast network, rail passengers have fallen from a 10 per cent share of traffic in 1970 to 6 per cent in 2001. This is not surprising when between 1990 and 1999 Europe saw its motorway network *increase* by 25 per cent.

Railways offer the convenience of centrally located stations and relative ease of travel. However the UK has experienced a lack of investment in the railway network for many years compared to Europe. European services run faster and operate more frequently. Eurostar destinations from London Waterloo include Paris, Brussels, Lille, Disneyland and Avignon. By connecting with local services, Eurostar makes it

possible to travel to other destinations, including Amsterdam, Bordeaux, Bruges, Lyon, Nice and Tours. The service from London travels via Ashford International terminal in Kent. Eurostar carries 64 per cent of all UK passengers travelling to Paris. The main difference between Eurostar and Le Shuttle is that Eurostar is a train with passenger carriages whereas Le Shuttle can transport cars, coaches and motorcycles complete with their passengers.

The most famous railway company is the Orient Express. The Venice Simplon Orient Express offers luxurious travel between London, Paris, Venice, Rome, Budapest, Vienna, Prague, Bucharest and Istanbul. The service runs between March and November. The traditional service from London to Venice lasts for two days with one night on board. The carriages reflect a golden age of train travel from the 1920s, the original carriages still being used. The Orient Express offers a scenic view of Europe coupled with the highest level of customer service and luxury.

In the United States Amtrak operates the national railway service. To travel from New York to Chicago takes 19 hours and to travel between New York and Los Angeles takes 66 hours. How does this compare with road and air travel? You will need to do research to answer this question.

A luxury railway carriage on board the Venice Simplon Orient Express

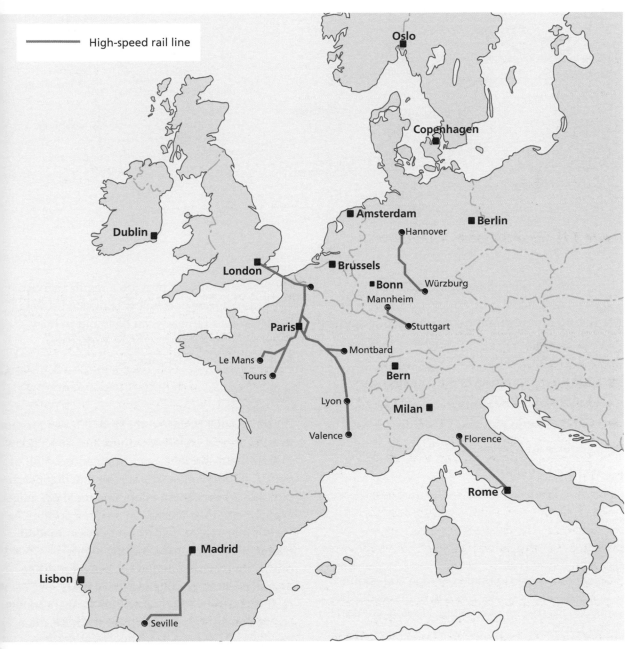

Figure 3.12 High-speed rail routes in Europe

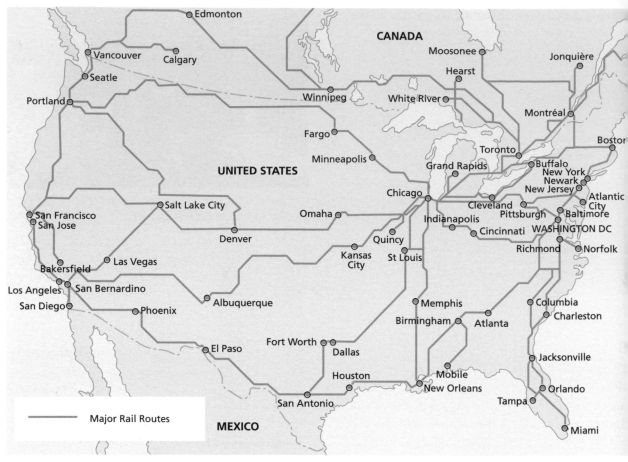

Figure 3.13 Major rail routes in North America

Scenic railways offer the tourist a unique experience of historic carriages and scenic beauty. Most only run during the summer months and are very popular, so booking is essential. In the United States examples include:

* Cass Scenic Railroad in the Appalachian Mountains, West Virginia

* Grand Canyon Railway, Colorado

* Cumbres and Toltec Scenic Railway, Rocky Mountains, Colorado.

Skills practice

Select one scenic railway in Europe and another in North America. Describe the route taken, the attractions that can be visited, levels of comfort and prices.

Underground railways provide a regular service with ease of transport below congested streets. Underground railways can be found in busy cities, including London, New York, Paris, Montreal and Amsterdam.

Air

Air travel is the preferred method of travel for most tourists. It offers relatively quick and direct access to short-haul and long-haul destinations. Half of the UK population makes at least one flight each year and 20 per cent of all international passengers begin or end their journey in a UK airport.

With the recent reductions in the number of people flying long haul and the highly competitive market that exists between airline operators, strategic alliances have been established between rival airlines to share routes and to cut costs. The major global airline alliances are shown in Table 3.2:

Table 3.2 Major global airline alliances

STAR ALLIANCE	ONEWORLD	SKY TEAM	KLM/NORTHWEST
Air Canada	Aer Lingus (Eire)	Aeromexico	KLM (Netherlands)
Air New Zealand	American Airlines	Air France	Northwest (USA)
All Nippon Airways	British Airways	Alitalia	
Asiana Airways	Cathay Pacific	Czech Airlines	
Austrian Airlines Group	Finnair	Delta Airlines	
bmi (British Midland)	Iberia	Korean Airlines	
Lufthansa	Lan-Chile		
Mexicana	Qantas		
Scandinavian Airlines (SAS)			

Budget airlines

There has been a tremendous growth in *budget airlines* during the last five years. Their success has been attributed to offering cheap regular flights to popular destinations. The recent success has been based on the following conditions:

* Using the most economical aircraft

* Not offering an in-flight service, reducing cabin staff and cleaning costs

* Reducing leg room whilst complying with government safety regulations

* Flying to popular destinations but avoiding routes dominated by major airlines

* Making efficient use of the aircraft flying several trips every day.

In the United States, Southwest Airlines is the largest budget airline, handling over 60 million passengers each year and flying to 60 US destinations. Other US budget airlines include AirTran Airways, JetBlue and Frontier. In Canada, WestJet and JetsGo offer budget flights.

In the UK, Ryanair and easyJet have dominated the market. Ryanair discovered that by reducing its ticket prices by half, compared to the major airlines, passenger numbers dramatically increased. Fares to some destinations in Germany are 80 per cent cheaper than those offered by Lufthansa and as a result the airline carries over 2 million passengers to Germany each year. Ryanair flies to 155 destinations in 17 European countries, including: Austria, Belgium, Denmark, England, Finland, France, Germany, Ireland, Italy, the Netherlands, Northern Ireland, Norway, Portugal, Scotland, Spain, Sweden and Wales. Of the 29 million passengers that fly with Ryanair, 43 per cent are leisure passengers, 36 per cent are visiting friends and relatives (VFR) and 21 per cent are travelling on business. France is the most popular destination for UK budget airlines. Ryanair flies more passengers to France than Air France.

In comparison easyJet operates from 55 airports, offering 180 routes. The airline carries 24 million passengers each year with 8.75 million of these originating from the UK. Other major UK budget airlines include: bmibaby, Flybe and MyTravelLite.

Skills practice

1 Using a selection of budget airline websites, identify the main routes taken by travellers from the UK.

2 Why have the budget airlines been so successful?

3 What strategies are being used by the major airlines in order to compete with the budget airlines?

Airports

UK airports handle approximately 190 million passengers each year; this figure is expected to grow to between 350 and 460 million by 2020. Heathrow is the busiest UK airport, handling over 63 million passengers each year, which accounts for approximately 40 per cent of air passengers in the UK. Gatwick Airport handles over 30 million passengers each year. However, the two largest airports are under increasing competition from the growth of regional airports. Airports offer a wide range of services, including retail, restaurants, ticketing, car parking and accommodation.

Airports also allow passengers to transfer between flights. Many airports are regarded as *hubs*, places that receive connecting flights from many destinations, allowing passengers a flexible combination of routes. Regional airports may not always offer a direct flight to a chosen destination, but instead offer a route that requires a transfer at another airport. These can be more expensive than travelling direct.

Due to the expansion of air travel in the UK the new Terminal 5 at Heathrow will add extra capacity. Stanstead Airport in Essex continues to expand and is the fastest growing airport in Europe; British Airports Authority (BAA), which owns the airport, is planning to double its capacity to 50 million passengers a year. There are plans to add a third runway at Heathrow between 2015 and 2020 with a second runway at Gatwick after 2019.

Regional airports offer local convenience with less congestion and cheaper car parking. Regional airports that continue to expand include the following:

Table 3.3 UK regional airports

REGION	AIRPORTS
The Midlands	Teeside, Birmingham
North of England	Manchester, Liverpool John Lennon, Carlisle, Newcastle
Northern Ireland	Belfast International, Belfast City, City of Derry
Scotland	Edinburgh, Aberdeen, Dundee
South-East	Luton, Norwich, Southampton, Southend, Kent International Airport, Lydd, Shoreham and Biggin Hill
South-West	Bournemouth International, Bristol International, Exeter, Newquay
Wales	Cardiff

Skills practice

1 Visit the British Airports Authority (BAA) website http://www.baa.co.uk and identify the services they offer to passengers.

2 Visit a regional airport website and identify the services that it offers to passengers.

3 Suggest why regional airports are handling increasing numbers of passengers.

In 2003 the world's busiest airports were the following:

Table 3.4 The world's busiest airports in 2003

RANK	AIRPORT (AIRPORT CODE)	LOCATION	TOTAL NUMBER OF PASSENGERS
1	Hartsfield-Jackson Atlanta International Airport (ATL)	Atlanta, Georgia	83,578,906
2	O'Hare International Airport (ORD)	Chicago, Illinois	75,373,888
3	London Heathrow Airport (LHR)	London	67,343,960
4	Tokyo International Airport (HND)	Tokyo	62,320,968
5	Los Angeles International Airport (LAX)	Los Angeles	60,710,830
6	Dallas-Fort Worth International Airport (DFW)	Dallas-Fort Worth, Texas	59,412,217
7	Frankfurt International Airport (FRA)	Frankfurt	51,098,271
8	Charles De Gaulle International Airport (CDG)	Paris	50,860,561
9	Schipol Airport (AMS)	Amsterdam	42,541,180
10	Denver International Airport (DEN)	Denver, Colorado	42,393,693
11	McCarran International Airport (LAS)	Las Vegas, Nevada	41,436,571
12	Sky Harbor International Airport (PHX)	Phoenix, Arizona	39,493,519
13	Barajas International Airport (MAD)	Madrid	38,525,899
14	Don Muang International Airport (BKK)	Bangkok	37,960,169
15	John F. Kennedy International Airport (JFK)	New York	37,362,010
16	Minneapolis Saint Paul International Airport (MSP)	Minneapolis Saint Paul, Minnesota	36,748,577
17	Hong Kong (HKG)	Hong Kong	36,713,000
18	George Bush Intercontinental Airport (IAH)	Houston, Texas	36,490,828
19	Detroit Metropolitan Wayne County Airport (DTW)	Detroit, Michigan	35,199,307
20	Beijing (Peking) (PEK)	Beijing, China	34,883,190

Source: Airports Council International (2005)

Skills practice

1 From the list of the world's busiest airports above identify those that are in Europe and North America and locate these on a map.

2 Suggest why most of the world's busiest airports are located in the United States.

Sea

Because the UK is an island it has many *seaports*. Ferry companies are facing increasing competition from the Channel Tunnel and the budget airlines. In the mid-1990s two out of three passengers who travelled across the English Channel did so by ferry, since the start of this century two out of every three passengers who travel across the English Channel do so by air. Nine out of 10 UK ferry passengers travelling outbound from the UK go to France, the rest travel to the Netherlands, Belgium and Scandinavia.

The ferry companies are looking to expand and the port of Dover invested £70 million in four new ferry berths to enable growth of the next generation of *ro-paxes*, passenger car ferries that also have large freight handling capabilities. Dover handles 60 per cent of passenger traffic across the English Channel. Dover Harbour Board have also invested in new check-in booths to allow passengers and freight to be processed more quickly.

Skills practice

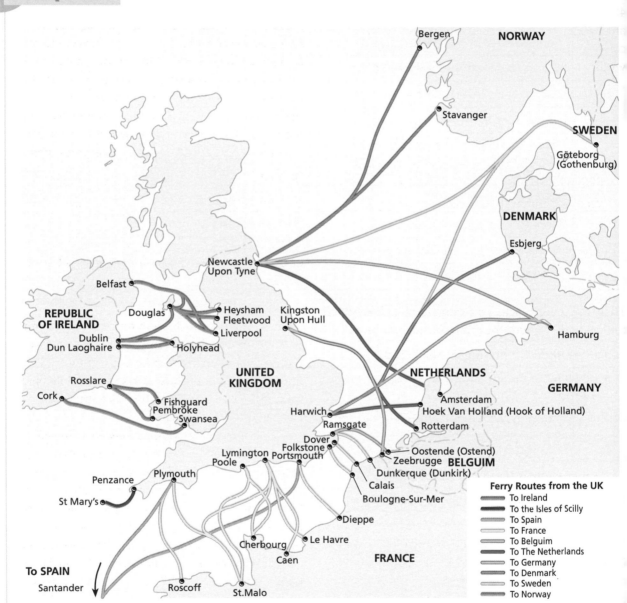

Figure 3.14 Ferry services routes from the UK

Using the map of ferry services from the UK, identify the routes taken by the following ferry companies:

- P & O Ferries
- Brittany Ferries
- Hoverspeed
- Sea France

Cruises

The UK is the second largest cruise market after the USA, with 940,000 cruise sales in 2003, a 14 per cent increase in sales on the previous year. The Mediterranean remains the most popular cruise destination in the world, although recently there has been growing interest in Northern European and Scandinavian cruises. The 55–65 age group dominates demand, with significant numbers in the 45–54 age group and the 65 plus. Older generations are attracted by the high quality of service and convenience of being aboard a luxury cruise ship whilst visiting a range of tourist destinations.

Skills practice

1 Using a range of cruise brochures identify the most popular itineraries in the Mediterranean.

2 Using the cruise brochures, identify the most popular itineraries in North America.

3 What are the main attractions of taking a cruise holiday?

Factors affecting tourist choice of travel method

There are several factors affecting tourist choice and the method of travel; the main considerations are:

* Cost of travel, including en-route costs
* Convenience for the nature of the group travelling
* Distance to be travelled, including journeys to airports
* Amount of time available for the journey, including check-in times at airports
* The purpose and duration of the visit
* Comfort, convenience and facilities offered.

Costs are an important factor to consider because in times of a recession spending on leisure and tourism is one of the first areas where savings can be made. The cost of a holiday is not just the cost displayed in the brochure. There are hidden costs such as entrance fees, food and drink, souvenirs and buying goods and clothes for a holiday.

Convenience can include date and time of travel and also the location of gateways. Airports and seaports that are at a long distance from home are less appealing than those that are closer to home and require less effort to get to.

The amount of time available for a holiday is also another important factor. A week's holiday might be better spent in a short-haul destination rather than a long-haul destination due to the amount of time spent travelling. This will also depend on the purpose of the visit. The three main purposes of visits are: leisure, business and visiting friends and family (VFR).

Levels of comfort and expectation may be reflected in the price, for example travelling on a budget airline compared to a traditional airline.

Tourists will often use a variety of types of transport to get from home to their final destination. This will depend on their preferred method of transport, on convenience, price, level of comfort and speed of travel. Examples include:

* Taxi
* Scheduled bus service
* Hire car
* Use of own car
* Accepting a lift from a friend or member of the family
* Rail.

Even within the destination tourists have a choice of transport available. They may prefer to stay within the destination and explore on foot. They may decide to use a hire car, taxi, local bus or train service or travel on the bus excursions chartered for the tourists.

Choices made by tourists may also change because the tourists themselves are changing. Increased travel and advances in technology bring about changes in expectation and level of service. Independent travellers, those not travelling as part of an organised package holiday, account for 55 per cent of the holiday bookings market. Between 1998 and 2004 the number of independently booked holidays increased by 60 per cent. This growth has been helped by the availability of low-cost travel and an increased use of the Internet in making bookings and researching potential destinations. UK tourists are not just seeking beach holidays but coupled with an increase in the short break market, they are increasingly seeking to experience different cultures and explore local heritage.

1 Why do people working in the travel and tourism industry need to know where major destinations are?

2 Can you name and locate the major continents and oceans on a map?

3 Can you name and locate the major tourist destinations and cities in Europe and North America?

4 Can you describe the climate of major destinations in Europe and North America?

5 Can you name some of the natural and built tourist attractions in Europe and North America?

6 Give examples of some of the tourist facilities found at major travel destinations.

7 Why are travel times and travel zones important to tourists?

8 What are some of the major travel routes across Europe and North America?

9 How would you go about researching information on a tourist destination? Give examples of primary and secondary sources that you would use.

10 Why do different types of people choose to visit different destinations as tourists?

11 What factors are significant in creating appeal to different types of tourists?

12 Describe the factors that affect future popularity and appeal of tourist destinations.

13 What are the different ways in which a tourist may travel to their destination?

14 Why is transport essential to the development of tourism?

15 Describe the factors affecting tourists' choice of travel.

UNIT ASSESSMENT

Portfolio practice

You have been asked to produce a portfolio of travel information for different types of customers travelling from the United Kingdom to two contrasting destinations: one in Europe and one in North America.

Your portfolio should contain:

- Information about the location of each destination, its landscape and climate.

- The script for a welcome meeting at each destination, linking the tourist facilities and major attractions to different customer types.

- Research into and analysis of the choice of methods of travel to each destination and travel while at the destinations, including appropriate maps.

- Recommendations to potential customers based on an evaluation of the appeal of each destination, and an evaluation of its likely future potential.

The welcome meeting

A holiday representative, or 'rep', delivers a welcome meeting to inform holidaymakers about local facilities and attractions. Part of the welcome meeting is for the holiday rep to make the attractions appear as exciting as possible so that the holidaymakers will want to visit them and get the most from their holiday. The holiday rep also acts as a sales person and will offer to arrange various visits and excursions to the most popular sites. The holiday rep must be able to identify what makes these attractions popular and understand which types of tourist they would attract by suggesting appropriate visits and excursions to the holidaymakers.

We have chosen Sorrento as an example of a European tourist destination and Los Angeles as an example of a North American tourist destination, and produced the following account of the areas, incorporating the sort of information that will be required for your portfolio. The same treatment will be required for whatever destinations you choose.

Sorrento, Italy

Information about the location of the destination, its landscape and climate

Sorrento has been a popular tourist destination since the 18th and 19th centuries and is located on the south-west coast of Italy in the Campania region, overlooking the Bay of Naples. The town is situated on a headland jutting out into the sea known as the Sorrento Peninsula, which forms part of the Amalfi coastline and is described in many guidebooks as one of Europe's most beautiful coastlines.

Here you could draw a location map of your destination and the surrounding area.
In the case of Sorrento this includes the Amalfi coastline and the Bay of Naples.

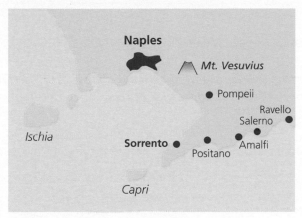

Figure 1 Location of Sorrento

Sorrento is a town built on a natural limestone cliff 60 metres (200 feet) above the sea. To the east are the limestone Lattan Mountains which rise steeply to heights of 1440 metres (5000 feet) and form the spine of the Sorrento Peninsula. The Amalfi coast is a dramatic landscape with a mix of steep mountains, forests and towns perched high on the cliffs. Amongst the mountains can be found olive groves, vines, almond and lemon orchards.

The northern side of the Bay of Naples, stretching round to the city of Naples, is a volcanic landscape dominated by the volcano Mount Vesuvius. The Bay of Naples itself provides a sheltered natural harbour with capes, bays, steep cliffs and tiny beaches.

Climate

Sorrento experiences a Mediterranean climate, the summers are long, hot and dry and the winter temperatures average at 10°C. Climate details for the nearest city of Naples (see table on page 128) demonstrate the average temperature, hours of sun and rainfall for the region:

Table 1 Climate information for Naples

Month	Average sunlight (hours)	Temperature (°C) Average		Record		Discomfort from heat and humidity	Relative humidity		Average precipitation	Wet days (+0.25 mm)
		Min	Max	Min	Max		am	pm	(mm)	(mm)
Jan	4	4	12	−4	20	−	77	68	116	11
Feb	4	5	13	−4	20	−	78	67	85	10
March	5	6	15	−4	25	−	77	62	73	9
April	7	9	18	1	27	−	79	61	62	8
May	8	12	22	3	32	−	85	63	44	7
June	9	16	26	7	35	Moderate	75	58	31	4
July	10	18	29	11	36	Medium	73	53	19	2
Aug	10	18	29	13	37	Medium	74	53	32	3
Sept	8	16	26	8	34	Moderate	78	59	64	5
Oct	6	12	22	3	29	−	79	63	107	9
Nov	4	9	17	−2	26	−	81	68	147	11
Dec	3	6	14	−4	20	−	80	70	135	12

Source: BBC Weather Centre (2004)

Italy is one hour ahead of Greenwich Mean Time; when the time is 4 pm in London it is 5 pm in Italy.

The following information will be useful to assist you in writing a script for a welcome meeting linking the tourist facilities and major attractions to different customer types

Attractions

With a wide choice of mountains, beaches, cities, historical sites and museums there is plenty to see and do. Staying in Sorrento itself offers a variety of activities and also a perfect base to travel to many other major attractions and sites, including the Amalfi Coastal Drive, the Roman ruins at Pompeii and Herculaneum, the city of Naples and the islands of Capri and Ischia.

Sorrento

Sorrento first began to find popularity as a tourist resort in the early nineteenth century and it still retains its small town charm. The resort attracts many English, German and Italian tourists. Although the town has no beach there are *stabilimenti*, which are piers that jut out into the sea upon which loungers and umbrellas can be hired for sunbathing and relaxing in the summer sun. The town comes alive at dusk for the daily *passeggiata* when visitors and locals stroll through the small streets browsing at the souvenirs and shops and stopping for a drink or meal in the bars, pubs and cafés. Sorrento is famous for intricate handcrafted woodwork gifts and also *limoncello*, an alcoholic drink made from lemons that are grown locally.

Sorrento

Amalfi coastal drive

This famous coastal road covers 80 kilometres (50 miles) and includes a series of hairpin bends and dramatic views. The coastal drive includes the historic towns of Salerno, Ravello, Amalfi, Positano and Sorrento that cling to the sides of the cliffs. From the coastal road beautiful gardens, vines, olive, almond and lemon trees can also be seen.

Pompeii, Mount Vesuvius and Herculaneum

For visitors who are interested in Roman history or are interested in finding out about the geology of the area, a visit to Pompeii, Herculaneum and Mount Vesuvius is recommended. Both Pompeii and Herculaneum can be accessed easily from Sorrento via the *Circumvesuviana* railway or by attending one of the many organised day excursions.

Situated in Ercolano, 12 kilometres (7.5 miles) south of the city of Naples, Herculaneum is much smaller but better preserved than Pompeii. The town was covered in 20 metres (6 feet) of mud after the eruption of Vesuvius in 79AD. A small area has been excavated allowing visitors to walk through the streets and see well-preserved houses and shops. Visitors can learn about the horrors of the eruption as people fled and were trapped between the hot gaseous mud and the sea.

Pompeii is the much larger and more famous of the two archaeological sites. Although the buildings are not as well preserved as at Herculaneum, Pompeii offers the visitor a wider view of Roman life, with shops, houses, streets, amphitheatres, the Forum, baths and a gladiator arena. The town was destroyed when a rain of ash buried it followed by the *pyroclastic flow*, a devastating collection of ash, rock and other material that flowed like an avalanche, covering the whole town. Pompeii first started to be excavated in 1748 and the finds of the excavations are on display in the National Archaeological Museum, *Museo Archeologico Nazionale*, in Naples.

If the towering volcano that dominates the skyline impresses the visitor then it is important to visit the source of the disasters, Mount Vesuvius. The volcano can be accessed from Pompeii by catching one of the buses outside of the *Circumvesuviana* railway station or by taking part in one of the organised excursions. The volcano is 1281 metres (4200 feet) tall and the last eruption was in 1944. There are basic tourist services at the car park before embarking on the half-an-hour climb to the crater along a gravel path. The view from the top overlooking the Bay of Naples is breathtaking. The view of the crater is also dramatic as small clouds of vapour can often be seen escaping. The volcano is still active and potentially could erupt at any time, however the volcano is being monitored 24 hours a day by a team of scientists and their observatory is open to visitors during the morning. Mount Vesuvius and the surrounding countryside is recognised as a National Park, providing a unique environment for wildlife.

City of Naples with Mount Vesuvius in the background

Naples

The city of Naples contains many attractions. It is a bustling city that offers historians, shoppers, children and many other tourists something to view and enjoy. The city is the capital of the region of Campania and is an area of complete contrasts. One of the most important attractions is the *Museo Archeologico Nazionale*, which houses one of the most comprehensive collections of Greco-Roman artefacts in the world, including sculptures, mosaics and artefacts from Herculaneum and Pompeii.

There are also many religious buildings to visit. One of the largest and most fascinating is the grand cathedral, the *Duomo*, which has undergone many alterations since being first built in 1272 and experiencing disasters such as an earthquake in 1456.

For the shopper Naples boasts that anything can be bought within the city, with most of the shopping being centred around the *via Toledo*. For the children Naples offers several castles, Europe's oldest aquarium, the *acquario*, which contains 200 examples of sea life found in the Bay of Naples, and the *Edenlandia* funfair.

The city does have a reputation for street crime and care should be taken around the central

City of Naples

station, *Stazione Centrale*. Naples can be accessed from Sorrento via the *Circumvesuviana* railway, by local bus service or on one of the organised coach excursions.

The Islands of Capri and Ischia

The two islands can be found off the Sorrento coast.

Capri has many picturesque towns and villages, quality restaurants, cafés, designer shops and narrow streets. It has been associated with rich and famous celebrities who visit the island. Many of the restaurants display pictures of their famous guests. If the weather is fine, boat trips using small rowing boats are available to the *Grotta Azzurra*, the Blue Grotto. This is where a refraction of light off the walls of the cave creates a magical blue glow, and the reflection of light off the sandy bottom creates a silver glow combining to create a spectacular scene.

Island of Capri

Ischia, the largest of the local islands, has a collection of thermal springs, as the island is volcanic in origin. Long sandy beaches and fishing villages can be found in combination with forested mountains. The visitor can enjoy the beaches, shop in the resort and drink the locally produced wine for which the island is renowned, or be pampered by spa treatments and take a dip in one of the thermal spas during the summer.

Activities

Events

Sorrento's patron saint *Sant'Antonio* is remembered on 5 February each year with processions and a large market. There are also a series of Easter processions that draw large crowds from neighbouring towns.

In July–August Sorrento hosts a series of classical music concerts, which is popular with tourists and local people.

The Sorrento Film Festival takes place in late November and early December and is regarded as one of the most important celebrations of Italian cinema in the country.

Food, drink and entertainment

The food is typically Italian with lots of pasta and pizza and famous Italian ice cream. *Limoncello* is a favourite drink with visitors. Local wine is also of good quality, the red wine *Lacryma Christi* being produced from grapes grown on the side of Mount Vesuvius. An evening stroll along the *via Cesareo* is part of local tradition as the town comes to life during the early evening into the night.

The *Teatro Tasso* theatre offers a range of local musical shows that appeal to visitors wishing to experience Italian music and culture. Local music is performed on a regular basis, which is considered to be more authentic than what is performed during Italian 'theme-nights' in tourist bars and hotels.

The popularity of Sorrento as a UK holiday destination is reflected in the presence of the *Circolo dei Forestieri*, the Foreigners' Club, where each night British people can be seen drinking British beer in an Italian setting with live music.

Accommodation

One of the most exclusive hotels that is a landmark in the centre of Sorrento is the *Grand Hotel Excelsior Vittoria*. Located on the site of an old Roman villa, it has been owned by the Fiorentino family since it opened in 1834 and has some of the best local gardens and terraces that overlook the Bay of Naples. There are plenty of 4-star and budget tourist hotels in Sorrento as well as a youth hostel, the *Ostello delle Sirene*. Campsites are also available to the west of Sorrento, which are easily reached via the SITA bus service from the railway station.

> *You will need to do research into and an analysis of the choice of methods of travel to the destination and travel while at the destination, including appropriate maps*

Travel to Sorrento

From the UK the most common method of travel to Sorrento is by air, arriving at Naples' *Capodichino* Airport. Flights can be taken from Aberdeen, Belfast, Birmingham, Blackpool, Bournemouth, Bristol, Cambridge, Cardiff, East Midlands, Edinburgh, Exeter, Gatwick, Glasgow, Heathrow, Humberside, Leeds/Bradford, Liverpool, London City Docklands, Luton, Manchester, Newcastle, Norwich, Southampton, Stansted and Teeside. Visitors on package holidays are usually transferred to Sorrento by coach; alternatives include using airport buses or the local *Circumvesuviana* railway service. Tourists can hire cars at the airport providing they have their driving license and insurance details.

A direct flight to Naples takes approximately two hours, with a coach or taxi transfer to Sorrento taking one hour, depending on traffic. Most of the scheduled flights that fly direct to Naples from the UK are dominated by the British Airways service from Gatwick. Recently other carriers such as Alitalia, easyJet and bmi have included scheduled services. As Sorrento is a popular package holiday destination many chartered airlines operate from regional airports across the UK.

Naples also has frequent rail connections with the rest of Italy via the *Stazione Centrale*, including hourly trains to Rome, a journey which takes between two and three hours. There are coach services to Naples from all other major cities in Europe and there is a London to Naples direct coach, run by National Express Eurolines.

Arrival by car in the region is possible via Italy's motorways, all of which are toll roads. From the north this would involve travel on the E45/A1 and then A3 or A16/A30 from the east.

Travel in and around Sorrento

The centre of Sorrento is easily accessible. There are local buses that operate along the Sorrento peninsula; these are orange in colour and run daily every 20 minutes until 8 pm. Longer distances can be made on SITA buses which are blue; these travel further along the Amalfi coastline. Tickets for SITA buses can be bought from places that display the SITA sign, including bars and shops near bus stops.

Trains run from Sorrento to Naples via stops such as Ercolano and Pompeii on the *Circumvesuviana* railway line. Tickets can be purchased at the railway station and the trains run approximately every 20 minutes from 5 am until 10.30 pm, and later at the weekend during the summer season.

Hydrofoil and ferry services operate between Sorrento, Naples, Ischia and Capri on a daily basis and timetables can be obtained from the port in Sorrento or from local hotels.

Taxis tend to be expensive in the region, so if travel by car is preferred then car hire from the airport or in resort would be advisable. However driving in Naples is not for the inexperienced.

> **The following are recommendations to potential customers based on an evaluation of the appeal of the destination and an evaluation of likely future popularity**

Sorrento and its surrounding area is popular with honeymoon couples, the older traveller and family groups. Italian food and culture is popular in the UK, so to experience an authentic Napolitana pizza in Naples and surrounding areas is part of the attraction. The town has a romantic charm with small shops, cafés and views over the Bay of Naples. The area also has many designated coastal walks for the active holidaymaker.

The ruins at Pompeii are well known and give a chance to explore Roman history at first hand. Naples provides the visitor with the historic charm and the hustle and bustle of a busy city.

Over 2,500,000 UK tourists visit Italy each year and stay for an average of 4.3 days, with longer stays in the south of Italy. The southern region of Italy is also experiencing a modest growth in the number of tourists. The north of Italy, in particular cities offering art and cultural attractions, are doing less well, mainly due to a reduction in the number of German and American tourists.

Approximately 8 per cent of Italy's inbound tourists originate from the UK, 8 per cent from France, 22 per cent from Germany and 12 per cent from the USA. The Italian tourism industry makes an annual profit of approximately €13.1 billion (£9.49 billion).

The hotel sector has seen a decline in the number of people staying by 1.4 per cent, but alternative accommodation, including farmhouses, hostels, and guesthouse accommodation, has seen an increase of 3 per cent. However, visitors from the UK prefer hotel accommodation rather than other types of accommodation; Naples alone offers over 28,500 hotel rooms.

Italian tourism is facing increasing competition from other Mediterranean destinations, such as Turkey, Bulgaria and Croatia which offer beach and cultural holidays at a cheaper price. However, the warm climate and extensive coastline in the south of Italy offers a strong potential for future development. The tourism market may have reached a stage of maturity in Sorrento but the potential for future development in terms of business, cultural and historical attractions are favourable.

For the latest travel advice to Italy visit the Foreign and Commonwealth Office website http://www.fco.gov.uk.

For further information visit:

Italian State Tourist Board http://www.enit.it

Italian State Tourist Board in North America http://www.italiantourism.com

Visit Sorrento http://www.visitsorrento.com

Los Angeles, USA

Information about the location of the destination, its landscape and climate

Over 24 million people visit Los Angeles each year, known locally as LA or the City of Angels, after its Spanish ancestors. Los Angeles is home to approximately 17 million people. It is a sprawling metropolis, a mega-city, that has grown so large that it is made up of 5 districts and 88 towns. It is the second largest city in the USA.

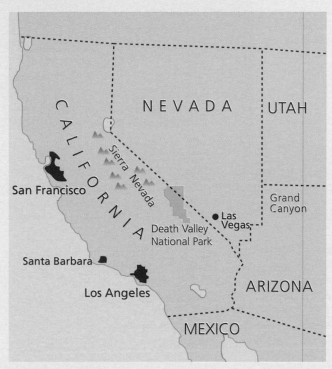

Figure 2 Location of Los Angeles

Los Angeles is in the state of California on the west coast of America. The state of California covers an area of 404,710 square kilometres (156,260 square miles), one-and-a-half times the size of Great Britain, and has 2000 kilometres (1250 miles) of coastline. The sandy beaches are located in the south with a more rocky and dramatic coastline towards the north. Inland the landscape is dominated by large mountain ranges that run north to south in line with the Pacific coast. In the east the Sierra Nevada mountain range reaches heights of 4000 metres (13,000 feet). The landscape features steep-sided valleys and large waterfalls.

Between the mountain ranges is Central Valley, which is 600 kilometres (372 miles) long and 60 kilometres (37 miles) wide. The San Joaquin and Sacramento rivers flow through the valley into the sea at San Francisco Bay. Further south are the desert valleys, including Death Valley, a dried salt lake that is 87 metres (286 feet) below sea level, the lowest point on the surface of the Earth.

Along the centre of California is where the two continental plates, the Pacific and the North American, are slowly moving past each other. These parts of the Earth's crust move around 3cm a year. When they rub together there is a shudder, which results in an earthquake. There are approximately 10,000 minor earthquakes each year. A large earthquake is likely to occur within the next one hundred years, but scientists are monitoring the movement of the ground so advanced warning may be given.

Climate

Los Angeles has a Mediterranean-like climate with warm dry summers and cool damp winters. The topography of the land affects the type of climate of California. The San Gabriel Mountains to the north of Los Angeles influence the weather. Moist air moves inland from the Pacific Ocean and is cooled as it rises over the mountains. This cooling effect produces heavy rainfall on the west side facing the sea. The east side of the mountain is in a rain shadow and receives less rain.

Central Los Angeles

The north of California is cooler than the south. The cooler conditions are perfect for wine production, especially in the vineyards of the Napa Valley near San Francisco. In the southern deserts, July and August can be unbearably hot as temperatures in Death Valley can reach 122°F (50°C).

Table 2 Climate information for Los Angeles

Month	Average sunlight (hours)	Temperature (°C) Average		Record		Discomfort from heat and humidity	Relative humidity		Average precipitation	Wet Days (+0.25 mm)
		Min	Max	Min	Max		am	pm	(mm)	(mm)
Jan	7	8	18	−2	32	–	67	47	79	6
Feb	8	8	19	−2	33	–	74	53	76	6
March	9	9	19	−1	37	–	77	51	71	6
April	9	10	21	2	38	–	82	55	25	4
May	9	12	22	4	39	–	86	59	10	2
June	10	13	24	8	41	Moderate	87	58	3	1
July	12	16	27	9	43	Medium	88	55	0	0
Aug	11	16	28	9	41	Medium	87	54	0	0
Sept	10	14	27	7	42	Medium	82	52	5	1
Oct	9	12	24	4	39	–	75	49	15	2
Nov	8	10	23	1	36	–	62	38	31	3
Dec	8	8	19	−1	33	–	60	44	66	6

Source: BBC Weather Centre

Los Angeles is located in a geographical basin. As cool air falls into the basin it prevents air pollution from escaping. This causes a mixture of foggy conditions and air pollution known as smog. Smog can irritate people suffering with asthma. It is estimated that 70 per cent of air pollution in Los Angeles is caused by vehicle emissions, as approximately 7 million vehicles are used daily. The sea fog only stretches inland for a few miles but it does reduce the temperature by several degrees.

California is set on Pacific Standard Time, which is 8 hours behind Greenwich Mean Time, 3 hours behind New York and 2 hours behind Chicago.

Attractions

Visiting Los Angeles is an exciting experience. This vibrant and diverse city is a collection of separate districts, each with its own identity. The financial and administrative heart of Los Angeles displays many skyscrapers, reflecting the economic wealth of the city. This wealth is based on the growth of the service sector, high-tech industries and leisure industries, which are mainly linked to film and the movies.

In Downtown Los Angeles, the Civic Center hosts a collection of governmental and federal buildings. Civic Hall is a large white tower 28 stories high that was made famous as the Daily Planet building in the film *Superman*.

Walt Disney Hall is an impressive metal structure that is shaped to resemble the opening of a rose and is the home of the Los Angeles Philharmonic Orchestra. The Museum of Contemporary Art (MoCA) contains a range of exhibits, including pop art, photography and multimedia shows. There are musical performances, which are usually free of charge. The Cathedral of Our Lady of the Angels (OLA) is a large modern Catholic cathedral set amongst a large plaza, gardens and a conference centre. It can hold up to 3000 worshippers with an interior larger than a football field.

El Pueblo de Los Angeles is a 44-acre historic park on the north-eastern edge of Downtown and includes many of Los Angeles' first buildings that date back as early as 1818. It is near to Union Station and provides access to Chinatown, which is home to over 200,000 Chinese Americans. Little Tokyo is the Japanese equivalent to Chinatown; although smaller in size it has traditional gardens, shops, cultural centres and Buddhist temples.

Exposition Park is located a few miles south of Downtown. It hosts a range of museums and sports facilities. The Rose Garden stretches for 7 acres and is popular for walks and is an escape from the busy city. Popular museums include the Natural History Museum of Los Angeles County with rare dinosaur skeletons and an insect zoo with live exhibits, the Californian African American Museum and the California Science Center with interactive exhibits and a 3D IMAX Theatre. The Los Angeles Memorial Coliseum is famous for hosting the first Super Bowl in 1967 and two Olympic Games in 1932 and 1984. It is now the home of the University of Southern California football team.

Hollywood is famous for its movie and film industries which began in the 1920s. The famous Hollywood sign is perched on the hillside of Mount Lee on the edge of Griffith Park. The original sign dates from 1923 and was used to promote a housing development by spelling out the word 'Hollywoodland'. The sign was shortened and became famous worldwide through its association with the entertainment industry.

Griffith Park is another large green open space where families can relax and explore the Los Angeles Zoo, the Autry Museum of Western Heritage and the Griffith Observatory and Planetarium.

Hollywood, Los Angeles

West Hollywood is home to some of the trendiest nightclubs, bars and restaurants. Sunset Strip is part of Sunset Boulevard where many famous music and film personalities have lived and entertained. There are many film and television studios, and some offer free tickets to live shows. Famous studios include: Walt Disney Studios, NBC Television Studios, Universal Studios, Warner Brothers Studios, Paramount Studios and Sony Pictures, which owns Columbia and TriStar Pictures.

Hollywood Boulevard is one of Los Angeles' most famous streets. Lining the sidewalks are the names of over 2500 celebrities engraved in bronze stars. The Hollywood Entertainment Museum is a celebration of the Hollywood film industry and offers a chance to see original film sets and costumes, including the command bridge of the *USS Enterprise* from Star Trek and the bar from the television comedy *Cheers*.

North of Sunset Boulevard is Beverly Hills, with large mansion houses, designer boutiques and expensive restaurants centred on Rodeo Drive. Visitors can find out where celebrities live

Rodeo Drive, Beverly Hills

by taking one of the guided tours. Other local attractions include the Museum of Television and Radio, the Museum of Tolerance and the Museum of Jurassic Technology, which includes some weird and bizarre exhibits.

West of Beverly Hills is Westwood, another wealthy neighbourhood that also has a large student population as it is the home of the University of California Los Angeles (UCLA). Visitors are allowed on campus to visit the library, sculpture gardens, art galleries, museums and film school. To the north of Westwood is the Getty Center. It was the home of the famous multi-millionaire John Paul Getty and includes a collection of lavish art works and a research centre. Entrance is free to the public.

The coastline of Los Angeles is dominated by the Santa Monica Bay, which escapes most of the smog and the heat associated with Los Angeles. The resort of Venice offers a mix of local people: street performers, musclemen and women, surfers and skaters. It is known locally as Muscle Beach.

Its bohemian reputation attracts students, artists and hippies. Originally designed to resemble the canals of Italy's Venice as part of a theme park, the original theme park has disappeared but visitors can explore what remains of the open waterways.

Further north along the coast is the famous resort of Malibu, 44 kilometres (27 miles) of coastline that is home to some world-famous A-list celebrities. Large mansions are hidden away from the roadside and patrolled by security guards. However, many celebrity spotters hang out at local stores and cafés in the hope of seeing someone famous. Away from the beach is Malibu Creek State Park, once owned by the 20th Century Fox studios and which provided the setting for many of the Tarzan movies and for the classic wartime television show M*A*S*H. The park is open to the public and includes a lake, waterfalls and hiking trails.

Muscle Beach, Los Angeles

A visit to Los Angeles would not be complete without a visit to Anaheim, the home of Disneyland. Disneyland opened in 1955 and has set the standard for theme parks across the world. Popular attractions include Main Street, Adventureland, Frontierland, Fantasyland, Tomorrowland, and the usual Disney characters. The California Adventure is adjacent to Disneyland and is regarded as a separate park. It contains a range of new attractions that include California Screamin' and The Twilight Zone Tower of Terror™ for the thrill seekers, family adventure with Jim Henson's Muppet Vision 3D and fun for the children with Jumpin' Jellyfish and Princess Dot Puddle Park.

For visitors who wish to experience a different theme park, Knott's Berry Farm park offers several themed lands, but it is the roller coasters that are the main attractions. Knott's Berry Farm has also been recently extended with the opening of an adjacent water park, Soak City USA.

Activities

Events

Los Angeles hosts a whole range of festivals throughout the year, which have national, regional and local significance. Below is a list of just one example from each month of the year. Many other festivals and events can be found listed in the guide books and brochures:

January	1 January is the Tournament of Roses in Pasedena when spectators can see a parade of floral floats and marching bands on Colorado Boulevard (http://www.tornamentofroses.com)
February	The Academy Awards happen at the end of February when the Oscars are presented at the Kodak Theater
March	St Patrick's Day with a parade along Colorado Boulevard in Old Town Pasadena
April	Long Beach Grand Prix with Indy car racing around Shoreline Drive
May	Mid-May allows visitors to view the work of popular and potential local artists during the Venice Art Walk
June	Late June includes the hosting of the carnival-like Gay Pride Celebration, with parades and street stalls
July	4 July is Independence Day in the United States and LA hosts huge fireworks displays and festivities in many communities within the city
August	Nisei Week in Little Tokyo with a celebration of Japanese America, including traditional martial arts demonstrations, karaoke and Japanese performances
September	5 September is Los Angeles' birthday; there is a civic ceremony and street entertainment to mark the founding of the city in 1781
October	31 October is the traditional Halloween Parade in West Hollywood
November	2 November is the Dia de los Muertos (Day of the Dead) celebrations throughout East Los Angeles, with many Mexican traditions being upheld
December	1 December is the annual Hollywood Christmas Parade, with a procession of brightly lit floats to launch the first of many Yuletide events

Food, drink and entertainment

Whatever a visitor to Los Angeles wants to eat and however much they want to spend can be accommodated in the city. For the customer who doesn't want to spend a lot on food there are a large number of budget food providers, including coffee shops, delis, diners and drive-ins offering soups, omelettes, sandwiches and burgers. Some are restaurants open 24 hours a day.

There are many establishments offering California cuisine, American dishes and also Cajun food. California cuisine is more widely found in Los Angeles than the traditional American cuisine of steaks, ribs, baked potatoes and salads. California cuisine offers local ingredients that are grilled rather than fried. Cajun cooking offers a range of inexpensive spicy fish-based dishes.

Being a cosmopolitan city Los Angeles also offers food from around the world, and has Mexican, Latin American, Italian, Spanish, Greek, Japanese, Chinese, Thai, Korean, Indian, Sri Lankan and Middle Eastern restaurants, examples of which can be found in each district. Vegetarian restaurants are to be found across the city but mostly in Westside.

Los Angeles has many bars available where you can get a drink. Each district of the city has its own types of establishment, ranging from beachside bars to cocktail lounges. Smoking is banned in most establishments under California law. If a traveller wants a bar-like atmosphere but no alcohol then one of the famous coffee houses is worth a visit.

Evening entertainment is widely available in Los Angeles, with a huge variety of pursuits available, ranging from clubs and discos, live music, comedy and theatre, to film. It is recommended when searching for entertainment and the trendiest nightclubs to look in local newspapers such as the *LA Weekly* or the *Los Angeles Times*.

Live music is extensively available, with a choice of music venues throughout the city. There is a lively rock and revived punk scene as well as hip-hop, country, jazz, salsa and reggae music on offer in venues such as the Hollywood Palladium, the Cat Club, the Blue Saloon and many others.

Classical music is not so widely available. Opera is performed by the LA Opera and the Orange County Opera Pacific, both of which stage productions between September and June.

The city boasts a wide range of comedy clubs, including the Comedy Store and the Improvisation, both of which host famous comics and open-mike sessions for the rising stars of comedy.

There are many theatres hosting musicals and classics with all-star casts, including the Alex Theater and Pantages Theater. There is also a collection of fringe theatres which host smaller productions and experimental shows, including the Cast-At-The-Circle theatre and the Open Fist Theater.

Most major feature films will be released in Los Angeles before anywhere else and shown in one of the many movie houses in Westwood or Santa Monica Parade.

Accommodation

Los Angeles has over 100,000 rooms available. Choices range from basic budget motels, hostels, bed and breakfast inns and camping sites to world-class hotels.

Each neighbourhood and district has its own range of accommodation available, apart from campsites which are mostly found on the edge of the urban area along the coast and in the San Gabriel Mountains.

Famous celebrity hotels include the Beverly Hills Hotel on Sunset Boulevard and the secluded Hotel Bel-Air on Stone Canyon Road.

> *You will need to do research into and analysis of the choice of methods of travel to the destination and travel while at the destination, including appropriate maps*

Travel to Los Angeles

The quickest and easiest way for the UK tourist to reach Los Angeles is by flying direct to Los Angeles International Airport. A non-stop flight from London to Los Angeles takes approximately 11 hours. Carriers that operate non-stop flights include Air New Zealand, American Airlines, British Airways and Virgin Atlantic.

There are flights to Los Angeles from the following UK airports: Gatwick, Heathrow, London City, Bristol, Cardiff, Newquay, Plymouth, Southampton, Birmingham, East Midlands, Norwich,

Humberside, Newcastle, Teesside, Isle of Man, Liverpool, Manchester, Leeds/Bradford, Aberdeen, Edinburgh, Glasgow, Inverness, Belfast City and Belfast International. Most of these airports offer a direct service.

On arrival at Los Angeles International Airport tourists can travel by the use of a courtesy bus to various hotels, or by taxi, car rental or a free bus to the Metropolitan Transportation Authority (MTA) bus terminal from where buses can be caught to different parts of the city.

If a visit to Los Angeles is part of a wider tour of the United States, the city can also be reached via one of the many domestic flights from around the country. The city can be arrived at by Amtrak train, which has private cabins and dining cars, by bus using the Greyhound bus service, by driving a hire car or as a part of a fly-drive package.

Travel in and around Los Angeles

When travelling in and around Los Angeles public transportation is operated by the Metropolitan Transportation Authority (MTA), which runs a widespread bus and rail system throughout the city. Downtown and some neighbourhoods are also served by DASH minibuses and Santa Monica and western Los Angeles is served by the Big Blue Bus.

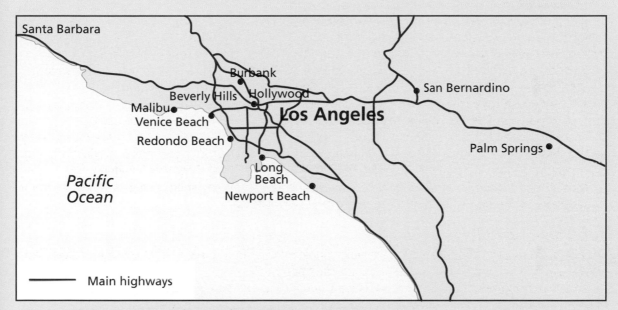

Figure 3 Main routes in and around Los Angeles

The following are recommendations to potential customers based on an evaluation of the appeal of the destination and an evaluation of likely future popularity

Los Angeles offers many attractions to families, student groups and independent travellers. Family groups will be attracted by the theme parks of Disneyland and Knott's Berry Farm and by the many film and television studios. Students will be attracted by the nightlife, the glamour of Hollywood and Malibu Beach.

Within any big city casual visitors are recommended to avoid certain neighbourhoods. Exploring Los Angeles by foot during the day is not a problem, but be extra cautious in East LA, Compton and Watts because of gang-related activity, and avoid them after dark. Poorly-lit side streets in Hollywood and Venice should also be avoided. Venice beach is notorious for criminal activities and as a result most areas of the beach are out of bounds after dark. However, areas such as Westwood and Beverley Hills and many of the other coastal resorts have lower rates of crime.

North America remains the most popular long-haul destination to be visited by UK residents. The threat of terrorist attacks has reduced the numbers of people travelling, although consumer confidence is returning, assisted by similarities in both culture and language. People in the UK are familiar with American culture through film, television, fashion and food.

Variations in economic performance and rising oil prices may affect the cost of holidays to the USA. Rising oil prices means that travel becomes more expensive. A slow down in economic growth means that people tend to spend less on their holiday and find cheaper alternatives, travelling to short-haul destinations rather than long-haul.

However, the exchange rate remains favourable for UK residents travelling to the USA. The average exchange rate for the US dollar in 1998 was $1.66 to the British pound and in 2002 the exchange rate was $1.50 to the British pound. This means that people travelling abroad can buy more for their money. Many consumer items in the USA are cheaper than in the UK.

For the latest travel advice to the USA, visit the Foreign and Commonwealth Office website http://www.fco.gov.uk.

For further information visit:

The Californian Division of Tourism http://www.visitcalifornia.com

LA Downtown visitors center http://www.lacvb.com

Santa Monica visitors center http://www.santamonica.com

Resources

Sorrento

Belford, R., Dunford, M. and Woolfrey, C. (2001) *The Rough Guide to Italy*. London: Rough Guides.

Hanley, A. (ed) (2000) *Time Out Guide: Naples Capri, Sorrento, and the Amalfi Coast*. London: Penguin Books.

Hatchwell, E. and Bell, B. (eds) (2002) *Insight Guides: Italy*. Singapore: APA Publications.

Leech, M. and Shales, M. (2001) *Globetrotter: Naples and Sorrento*. London: New Holland Publishers.

Simonis, D., Adams, F., Roddis, M., Webb, S. and Williams, N. (2002) *Lonely Planet: Italy*. London: Lonely Planet Publications.

Williams, R., Muscat, C. and Bell, B. (eds) (2001) *Insight Guide: Southern Italy*. Singapore: APA Publications.

Los Angeles

Campbell, J., Chilcoat, L., Derby, S., Greenfield, B., Heller, C.B., Martin, S., Miller, D., Morris, B., Ohlsen, B., Schulte-Peevers, A., Wolff, K. and Zimmermann, K. (2004) *Lonely Planet: USA*. London: Lonely Planet Publications.

Dickey, J.D., Edwards, N., Ellwood, M. and Whitfield, P. (2003) *The Rough Guide to California*. London: Rough Guides.

Lagrange-Leader, F. (ed) (2002) *Everyman Guides: California*. London: Everyman Publishing.

Teuschl, T. (2002) *Insight Compact Guide: California*. Singapore: APA Publications.

Wilcock, J., Zenfell, M.E. and Bell, B. (eds) (2001) *Insight Guide: Southern California*. Singapore: APA Publications.

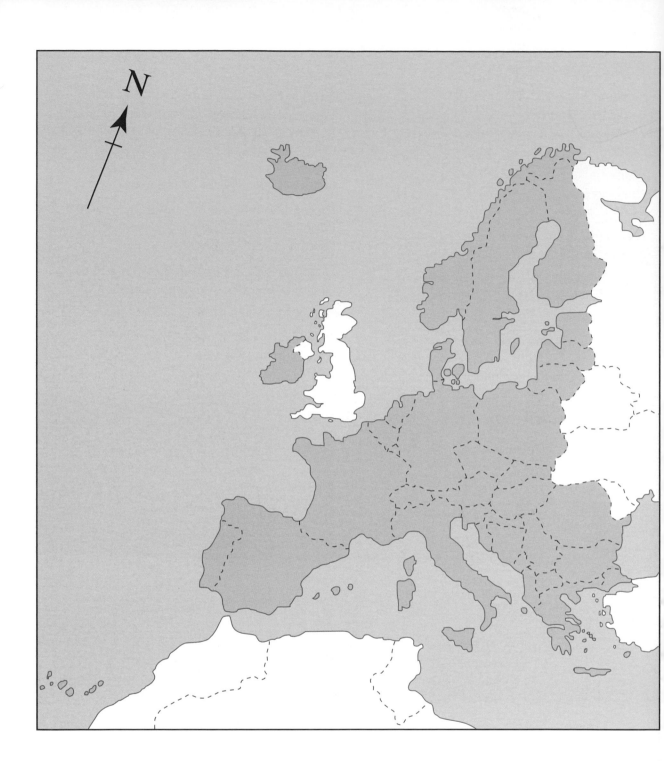

N

Index